Other Books By Love Life Lee

THE SCAFFOLDING OF LIFE

**The Wonderful World Of
Geometric Matter
The Building Blocks
Of All Biological Life &
Our Universe
Access The Blueprint In
Your DNA
Grow A Rainbow Light Body
Stop Karmic Cycles & Evolve
Transcend Time & Space &
Ascension You Will Achieve
BY
LOVE LIFE LEE**

The Scaffolding Of Life
The Building Blocks Of Sacred Geometry
Learn The Secrets Of Our Physical Universe &
Biological Makeup Of Our DNA, How To Evolve
Consciously Transcend Time & Space
To Learn How To Transverse The Universe With
Thought Mind Body & Spirit
Using Your Conscious Energy
Using Your Life Force Understand Your Full
Potential Grow A New Body Into Being
Consciously Evolve & Ascend
Create A Rainbow Body Of Light
Your Divine Right

Other Books By Love Life Lee

THE BIOLOGY & CHEMISTRY & MEDICAL FRAUD EXPOSED

& THE TRUTH OF BACTERIA & VIRUSES & ALKALISED HEALING OF THE BIOLOGICAL AVATAR BODY, MEANING THE COLLAPSE OF THE PHARMACEUTICAL INDUSTRY, THE WHOLE MEDICAL BASIS OF TEACHING STANDARD WILL COLLAPSE AS WELL AS UNIVERSITIES AND EDUCATION SYSTEMS, A NEW/ANCIENT NATURAL WAY TO HEAL, DIET IS KEY TO HAVE WELL BEING TO BE IN FULL HEALTH, TO EVOLVE ASCEND TRANSCEND TO BECOME ILLUMINATED TO ACCESS YOUR ETERNAL LIGHT BODY
BY
LOVELIFELEE

CHANGE YOUR MINDSET

THROUGH

The Eight Fundamental Principles Of Creation

Through Your Manifestation

Of

Animated Geomancy

Via

Meditation

To Access Your Eternal Light Body

BY
LoveLifeLee

PAGE INDEX AT BACK OF BOOK

Published in 2023 by FeedARead.com Publishing

Copyright © The author as named on the book cover.

The author or authors assert their moral right under the Copyright, Designs and Patents Act, 1988, to be identified as the author or authors of this work.

All Rights reserved. No part of this publication may be reproduced, copied, stored in a retrieval system, or transmitted, in any form or by any means, without the prior written consent of the copyright holder, nor be otherwise circulated in any form of binding or cover other than that in which it is published and without a similar condition being imposed on the subsequent purchaser.

A CIP catalogue record for this title is available from the British Library.

Other Books By Love Life Lee

Other Books By Love Life Lee

THE MOTHER SPIRIT OF AYAHUASCA MEDICINE

The Journey Of Shamanic Healing In Peru South America In The Garden Of Eden's Original Rainforest

The Mechanical Sciences, Medicinal Properties & Spirits Behind Ayahuasca The Medicinal Plant & The Holographical Hyper-Dimensional Matrix Of The Creation Built With The Super Advanced Biotechnology Of DNA Operated By Ultra Violet Energetic Eternal Spirit Consciousness

By
LoveLifeLee

Other Books By Love Life Lee

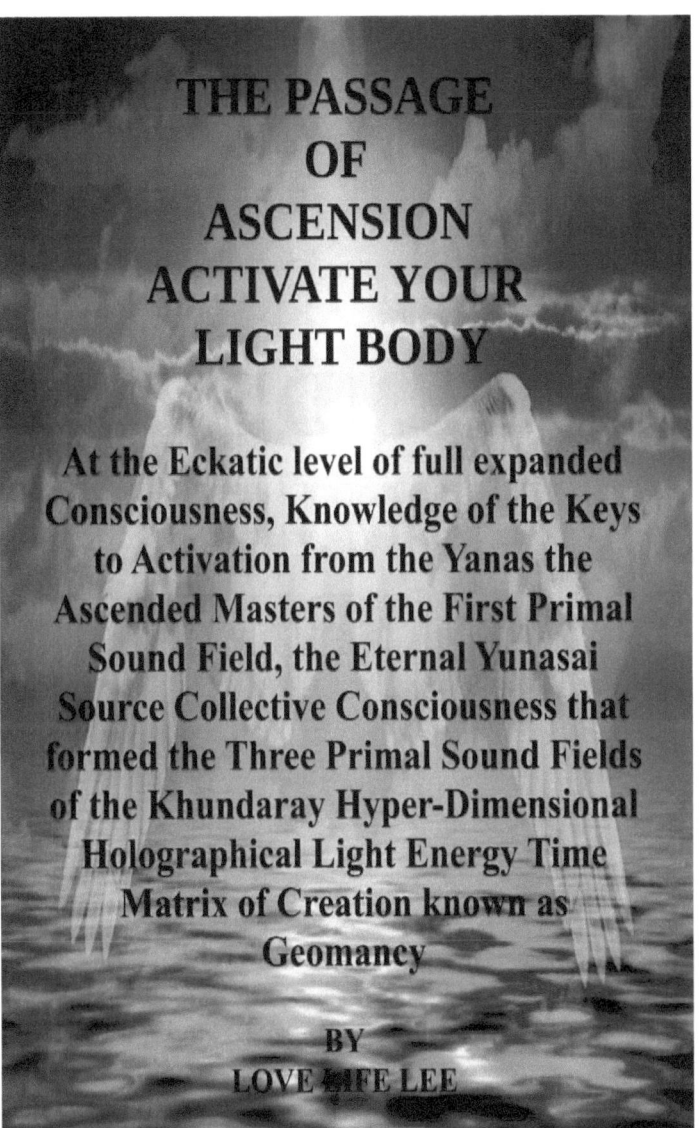

THE PASSAGE OF ASCENSION ACTIVATE YOUR LIGHT BODY

At the Eckatic level of full expanded Consciousness, Knowledge of the Keys to Activation from the Yanas the Ascended Masters of the First Primal Sound Field, the Eternal Yunasai Source Collective Consciousness that formed the Three Primal Sound Fields of the Khundaray Hyper-Dimensional Holographical Light Energy Time Matrix of Creation known as Geomancy

BY
LOVE LIFE LEE

Other Books By LoveLifeLee

The Mental Illness Of GENDER IDENTITY DISORDER

Known As GENDER DYSPHORIA

BY
LOVE LIFE LEE

The Eight Principles Of Creation

The Eight Principles Of Geomancy Of Sacred Geometric Animated Life Manifested By Eternal Spirit Source Light Beings Consciousness

Principle 1 – The Principle of Mentalism.
Principle 2 – The Principle of Correspondence.
Principle 3 – The Principle of Vibration.
Principle 4 – The Principle of Polarity.
Principle 5 – The Principle of Rhythm.
Principle 6 – The Principle of Cause & Effect.
Principle 7 – The Principle of Natural Law.
Principle 8 – The Generative Principle.

Also interlinked are the Law of Karma, the Law of Attraction, & Free Will.

CHAPTER ONE

The Hidden Knowledge Manifesting a New Mindset & The Eight Fundamental Principles Of Creation

To manifest a new Mindset you need to know the knowledge that has been hidden from humanity keeping them in bondage, this eternal Cosmic and Universal knowledge and wisdom must be shared with all of humanity, to move from the bondage of enslavement by the Elite thirteen bloodlines of the Brotherhood of the Snake, the Reptilian shapeshifting Humanoids that have suppressed humanity its entire history, keeping them in negative low vibrational Mindsets, there is a Moral obligation to share this fundamental knowledge with Humanity as a Collective. First lets look at the first Principles that are fundamental beginnings, Principle comes from the Latin word Principia, this means first, foremost, leading or most necessary, so it is that which matters most is the first things that must be perceived, comprehended and understood, before anything else can be understood. Principles have to come first but at this time by orchestration it puts shrievalties first, of administration and jurisdiction of illegal, corrupted, unlawful laws and policies from Statute Law, from the criminal Elite in power that suppress humanity in every facet and sphere of society, they have steered humanity away from the first Principles of Life and Creation. The first things first are the Eight Principles of Natural law, they are known in the Occult as the Hermeticism Principles, this is a complete version of the lost Principles, first is the Principle of Mentalism which states that, the all, everything in Creation is actually a manifestation of Mind, the always continuum of Mind. This means that everything that happens is a result of a mental projected state that proceeded it, so for anything to exist in the physical reality, thoughts came first that formed the surrounding material reality. You have to understand that you are an individual cell of Source, and that the Universe is a hologram of a mental construct, of Source energy. Thoughts lead to the manifestation of material things and events, thoughts create conditions, thought comes first, thoughts create our state of existence and the quality of our experiences, and on this Planet Gaia our thoughts interact with the electromagnetic field of the Planet to manifest physical matter. So therefore we must become individually responsible for our thoughts and what we think, on a twenty four hour daily basis. This is because it's the thought processes that are driving our behaviours from belief systems that we have created and embedded in the mind, that operate like a program, our thoughts and emotions are driving our actions. So to change our behaviour we have to change out thoughts and emotions because they are the driving force behind the behaviour, then our physical surrounding reality will change. So if you want a change your reality, you yourself have to change your thought process, your belief systems and your Mindset, other wise you will stay in the same reality because your thoughts are not conducive to the requirements to manifest and receive what you wish to have or experience. Most people have been programmed and conditioned to receive the opposite of what you wish to manifest, so this is the Principle of Mentalism.

The Principle of Correspondence states that which is above is similar or like to that which is below, meaning that which is below is like that which is above, meaning it is a mirrored effect, the above in this case is the macrocosm, which is the Cosmic Law of large things, these are the Laws that Govern the Creation, which we have been programmed to perceive as outside of ourselfs but we are the Universe. The macrocosm are the very large manifestations of matter and are the totality of everything, and the microcosm is the very miniture things, that are individual units that are comprised of the whole in their aggregate, because they are a reflection of each other, they cannot be separated from each other, as one goes, the other goes, because the Universe is a hologram, a holographical system, it is a mental image. When we pass a lazer though the hologram it projects a three dimensional image, even if it's a flat image, it is reflected back as a three dimensional image, and the reason its called a holistic image is because if you break the image into several pieces or components, it will still project the entire three dimensional image from only a section or piece of the Original Image, so if you have eight pieces of one image, it won't relect back as eight parts of an image, it will relect back eight whole complete images of the entire Original Image. So within the Universe everything is contained in the smaller parts, so one cell of the Creation can recreate the entire Creation with every Planetry body and every species that already exists within it. This is the Mental Universe reality we exist and live in, so the Universe is holographical in nature and the Universe is living inside each and everyone of us, and the Universe is like an individual body, we are a reflection of each other. Another part of the Principle of Correspondence is that the Creation and Universe is refractal in nature, so fractals are what create Geomancy, which is animated form build with Sacred Geometry at different resonances of light, which is what all Life is created from in geomentry, in algebra, in nature, that is what we call Animated Life of Existence. So fractals are self similar assembling mathematical generating patterns, we can perceive this is the Fibonacci Sequences, in mathematics, this is continually repeated throughout the Creation of

Nature. Looking at the structure of the atom which is a microcosm of our Bodies, the Solar System, the Galaxy, the Universe and the Cosmic Creation of which is the mirrored macrocosm. They all derive from the same patterned make up and all have an enveloping torus field, with a balanced dyamic fluctuating energy flow process, consisting of a single axis and two vortices, energy passes through one vortex along the centre of the axis, out the other vortex, then wraps back around the circumference and renews by passing through the Original Vortex. So they are all repeats of the same pattern, so the Universe is both holographic, meaning the Whole is contained within all parts, and vice versa its reversed in a converse manner with change of order or relation, reciprocally, with a reversed relationship, working in Union as One. And it is also a fractal Universe, so it is self similar across all scales of its entire Existence, this is the Principle of Correspondence.

The Pinciple of Vibration states that there is no such thing as rest, as dead or non motion. So we then can perceive that death is an illusion of the Minds belief systems, because a supposed true death would be the cessation of all motion and energy, this is not possible because all energy just transmutes into another form, or back to its original state of being. So you can't go anywhere in the Creation where something is at complete rest, everything moves, everything is osolating and vibrates, and at the most fundamental level the Universe every single thing or molecule which comprises it, is ultimately pure vibatory energy that is manifesting itself in different ways, different frequencies, different vibatory forms and states of matter. The Universe has no true solidity as such as we imagine to perceive when trapped in the mind of the matrix, solidarity at the macrocosmic level of matter is just energy in a state of vibration, so nothing is absolutely soild. So therefore we are Eternal Immortal (Spirit) Rainbow Light beings of Divine

Ultra Violet Energetic Angelic Consciousness from Source, the Conscious Energetic Field outside time and space in the Eternal realms, that has projected it's self outwards, to create this holographical Creation, for Eternal Spirit Conscious beings to become Animated in Geometric Light Form. So this means the entire Creation, all Cosmoses and Universes are Spirit, every cell is Spirit manifesting in Animated Form, via matter of which its structure, every cell of the building blocks of the cell has two opposing energies one in a state of rest, and the opposing force of energy in a state of of motion, this is the driving energy states and forces of the cells of matter, all created from electromagnetism, gravity and the strong and weak nuclear forces, its these fundamental energies or elements that create all Animated Life. So we can perceive that we are Spirit having a holographical projected experience, so that's how we can perceive the Principles of Vibration.

The Principle of Polarity states that everything has a dual nature to it, that there are polarities in everything that exists, that everything has poles and has its opposites, these opposites are actually identical in nature, but they are very different by degree. So to perceive this look at hot and cold they are the complete opposites, or we can look at it from an energy point of view, because they are the same thing just that the cold is missing some hot energy, and the hot is missing some cold energy. So we have to perceive it as the presence or absence of heat energy, they are the same thing energy, whether its concentrated in specific area to make it hotter, or whether its absence in a particular area making it colder, it is the same energetic force just shifting it polarities. So that's what hot and cold are at the fundamental level at our level of perception, they are opposites that at the fundamental level are the same thing, energy or its lack off, therefore extremes can meet and blend and interact with each other, like in Ancient Chinese knowledge, of the symbol of Life Force, the Ying and Yang symbol, representing the balanced flow of Life Force within of positive and negative, or dark and light or masculine and feminine. So they need to be blended and at some level of reality, everything that is seemingly contradictory may be reconciled and this is at the Unified Field level. So everything is Consciousness, Pure Consciousness, but at this level there are differences in Consciousness, and at this level of Consciousness we need to perceive it and totally understand it, so we can rectify the imbalances, so that we can manifest matter in the correct way, with morality.

The Principle of Rhythum states that everything flows out and in, everything has tides, all things rise and fall, so everything has a rythum to it or a swing to it between the two poles or polarities, So there are tendencies that exists within energy, as we know the pedulum swing under the influence of gravity manifests freely in everything we perceive and do in life. The pendulum has equal swing from the left and from the right, that are equal opposites of equal measurement, the rythum compensates itself, so in relation to Natural Law, many will say that's the way the tide or wind is taking us, or perceive that its just the way our tendancies are directing us, but this is not at all accurate, because nothing is solid or set in stone, frequencies, and rythum of energy are in motion on a continuum, just with one part in rest and the other part in motion. When we look at our ancestors of all humanities cultures they understood that these eight fundamental Principles, were about accessing higher levels of Consciousness, to connect to Nature, to Spirit, to the Universe and Creation, to evolve, to then transcend. They knew we can could attain higher levels of Consciousness via rythum, because rythum is a Principle, that has a tendancy to swing a certain direction, of the two poles, polarities of positive or negative, light or dark, good or evil, and masculine, male or feminine, female. So to overcome and control your own Inner rythum , you need to go with the flow of energy not against it, because your creating resistance, expending even more effort, even more energy, which will take you further away from the direction you wish to go, or create the surrounding reality you no longer wish to experience. So the Principle of Rythum in Natural Law of Cause and Effect, which we know are affects that are driven by causes that you know come first and then manifest conditions. So when we look at the Principles of Cause and Effect, it says that every cause has its effect and every effect has its cause, so that means everything that happens, occurs according to Principles of Law. This meaning when laws are not recognized the person or beings mind perceives it as consequences, when there is no such thing, chance and consequences are an illusion of the mind, in a certain belief system.

So then perceiving Free Will we can create on many planes of existence but all has to be manifested by the fundamental series of Cosmic Law, for nothing can escape it. Free will can ignore the laws but will have consequences in the Law of Karma, via the Law of Attraction, so there is no breaking of the eight fundamental Principles or Creation Laws without consequences. So Free Will is operating within the boundary conditions of the series of Natural Law, if Free Will goes past these parameters it breaks Natural Law with negative consequences, this is also known as consequentialism, and this knowledge is of how consequences are generated by our Free Will decision making processes, within the boundaries of Natural Law. The Free Will Consequentialism effect is not immediate in its manifestion, in this dimension we have a time delay, from the cause and motion effect, then the Universe will manifest Intelligently and provide you with what you manifested to experience. The Universe will arrange and rearrange to manifest what Consciously or UnConsciously you chose to experience, via your Cause and Effect of thought, emotion and feeling. So there is a time intermission between the cause of the mind the mental protection, and the effect the manifested animated physical surrounding reality that encompasses you. So the pattern recognition of the rythum of Cause and Effect is not perceived because of the separated delayed perceived linear time effect of manifested physical matter.

So if manifestation of our mind projections were instantly manifested and we were to harm another person, then we would instantly feel that pain, this is because of the Law of Attraction, so we would not repeat the same thought processes, but we would perceive, understand and recognize the pattern and stop that pattern of thought projection. But with the time delay that does not happen, so there is a delay before we get to experience something harmful to ourselves once we do something harmful to other people, so that is why it is very difficult for people to perceive the connection through the time delay. So this is why so many people are manifesting the opposite of what they really wish to manifest and experience, so we have to change our thought processes and its projections that manifest physical matter, and we need to control our emotions and behaviours. Then when we perceive that there is a plane of Cause and a plane of Effect, the two planes, we can then understand that no power to effect any change lies on the plane of effects, which is the physical manifested reality that envelopes us, so what already is, cannot be changed, so you cannot change the past, but you can change the out come of some of the present and completely change the future direction you wish to go and experience in the manifested form of Geomancy. So what is now in the present is truth of the reality we have manifested Individually and Collectively as a race, and at this time manifested our reality under negative influence, and programming that's been projected into the minds of humanity, by the Fallen Angels Collectives, the shapeshifting Brotherhood of the Snakes, we have to reject it or except it, and then focus our mental fortitude to manifest intentionally and directionally to attain our dreams and attain evolution in Consciousness. So the physical manifested world up to this moment has happened because of things that occurred in the past, from the causes that happened in the past. So the plane of Effects of the physical world is where manifested realities have already occurred, having already manifested in structure of Scared Geometric shapes, that have formed due to their underlying causal factors. Then the plane of Effects constitutes that within what has already occurred as such, no power to effect change lies here because that which has already occurred, and cannot be unoccurred, that which has occurred cannot undo itself, because it has already happened, it has become the reality of truth. At this present moment in the now, the human race has had its

Collective Consciousness manipulated to create a distorted negative reality for our race of humanity, and to keep us from evolving and ascending into Eternal Angelic Human Light beings, that is our fullest potential. So our Collective Consciousness has been influenced by gravish trickery by others, that do not have our best interests at heart, but their agendas are domination of the masses and the Planet, they want to see humanity trapped upon a plane of Effects in this lower density, that has left humanity ignorant of the underlaying causes, the causes that the individual has themselves set in motion, this leads to negative manifestations of self inflicted sorrow, sadness and suffering in their own lifes, while also possibly inflicting suffering on others simultaneously. So when your trapped in the Matrix of the Mind at this level or plane of Consciousness its because your only perceiving the symptoms. But when you can perceive the other plane of Causality which is the Mind, the psyche, the mental realm, the mental manifested reality, and according to the first Law of Mentalism the first Principle of Natural Law states, everything that manifests must first manifest in Mind before it can manifest physically in Animated Existence. So the plane of Causality is the Mental World that is generating the Causes in the Mind first, then it trickles down to the Physical plane, where it is manifesting physically after its manifested in the Mental World of the Psyche. So we can then perceive that the plane of Causality is where the causes are set into motion prior to those causes manifesting as formed realities in the plane of Effects.

So then we come to the seventh Principle of Natural Law which Law of Gender, which states that gender exists in everything, and everything has its masculine and its feminine components or Principles. This relates to the human brain, the Psyche, to Consciousness, to belief systems, so Gender manifests on all planes of Existence, mental, emotional, physical and Spiritual. So when we perceive mental gender, it is the state of coexistence between the masculine and feminine aspects of the Psyche, the Mind, our left hemispheres of the brain is what mostly facilitates the masculine anilitical brain of logic, with linear thought processes, but the right hemisphere of the brain facilitates the feminine aspects, like creativity, intuition and compassion by using holistic thought processes.

Then we come to another Hidden Principle, which is actually the eighth Principle of Natural Law, this Principle of Natural Law binds all the other Principles of Law together, it is the enveloping Principle or the encapsulating Principle, or the encompassing Principle, for it is the container inside which all the other Principles correspond in conformity in harmony, in balance, all Principles fit perfectly Union as One. So then we come to the the Cosmic refractal pattern of the Flower of Life, of the Seed of Life, that generates and grows, Creating and forming Life into Animated Form, the seed has its outer shell, then at the centre you have the creative genetic informatial material that's fragile, so the outer shell has to be solid to keep the DNA genetic coding information, and the Creative essence of that Species of Life, protected, as orchestrated by Divine design. So what is the Eighth principle of Life, it is the thing that has to be present in order for any change to manifest itself, and it is known as the Generative Principle or the Principle which actually Governs the Creation. That which is actually the causal factor that goes into effect and generates the result, that of what we think, say and feel, via our emotions, is the result of want we want to manifest and experience, and what is real. The Eighth Principle is the Generative Principle of Caring in the present moment of now, this Caring Principle has an underlying energy of Love. So now with that in Mind what are you focusing on in Life in your Mental Capacity, are you having moments of stillness and silence to gain clarity, and in turn direction, as you connect deeper into higher levels of perception of Conscious Awareness, connecting to Nature and Spirit, and learning to focus the Vibration of Love in all we manifest into physical reality in the Creation. Then our Love focused manifestations will be generated, created, and grown into Geomancy formed Animated Life. But we must perceive the negative not ignore it or more negativity will manifest through ignorance into Animated Form of a negative lived experience, because we are fuelling it by being ignorant, this then ensures that it becomes manifested in Animated Form. So we have to perceive the Eighth Principle of Caring, as vibrating from Love in the manifestations we are giving our Creative Energy to, the direction its focused upon, that we actually Love and Care about enough to spend out time on, as to what you actually want to put your focused attention on, as to what you want to have as an Animated Lived experience, in the Manifested Reality of this World and beyond inside the Whole of the Holographical Creation, and beyond in the Eternal realms of Spirit, the realms of Source. So it is the Eighth Principle of Caring which is the Principle of Love, that is generating our Lived experiences. But the reality is that most people in the aggregrate of our Collective race are so dulled down in Intelligence, and bombarded with violence, creating a State of Fear, and programmed and indoctrinated, that they don't care any more about Society, they have given up, lost faith, and forgotten the Inner Core Essence of what it is to be a Divine Spiritual being, that is manifesting in an Angelic Human Avatar, with access to only two strands of our twelve strands of DNA, keeping us in a low density of Consciousness. So when we are in the aggregrate of the Collective it is an impossibility to change the direction of energy, to change the direction of Consciousness, and to manifest what we say we wish for, this is just how the Law of Attraction works.

So the Eighth Principle is the dynamic of Caring or rather Love, what we Love and Care about on a day to day basis acts as the driving force of our thoughts and actions. So we need to focus on the heart and come from that space in manifestations, joining the Heart with the Mind in Union, and using and trusting our first brain our gut, but we need to have a high vibrational diet and feed the gut, the brain and body with the right nutrients so they function at there optimal levels, to gain rapid functions of processing of information, and to attain higher sensory functions and abilities. When we learn to Love and Care enough, then we can attain and develop the knowledge into understanding and then use it in practice. So the order they should be applied are from the Heart, then the Mind, then the Gut, then from Love of Caring, then from knowledge and wisdom, then from action. These are the three steps of the process that all have to be in place for us to experience Unity Consciousness, that's the heart that comes from Spirit, the Mind that is the second brain and the Gut that is the first brain. So Unity Consciousness is the Unifying of false emotions and actions, and the three aspects of Consciousness such that there is no contradiction between them. So what we think mentally in thoughts, and what we say vibrationally we want, and we think how we feel and how we act are actually one and the same, there's no contradiction. So care, knowledge and action, that is Unity Consciousness, and Love of Caring is the driving force of our thoughts and actions while manifesting physical matter form into reality. The Love of Caring energy force of Life is the Generator of our lived experience Individually and Collectively of the quality of our shared experience here on the Planet Gaia. So Love of Caring is what generates the Whole, the Brahman, the Creation, this is why it is called the Generative Principle. It has be paralled as like the heart, the pump, the generator of the body that's osilating life in Animated Form, as does the

Generative Principle osilate the Generator that provides energy for the Holographical Super Advanced Biotechnology of the Living DNA Creation, that vibrates it into being, into the Animated Sacred Geometic Form of Geomancy. So the heart pumps blood with Life Force in it and the Generative Principle pumps the energetic Life Force of the Creation, the heart generator is what pumps that through the whole Physiology and enables us to continue to Sustain Life. So it's the heart which is generating experience, because what we Love and Care about determines what our thoughts are, of what we are thinking about on a day to day basis, which in turn directs our actions of behaviour.

When we look at Freemasonary and their main symbol with the G in the middle, the G stands for the Generative Principle of Geomancy, which is manifested Animated Life, at their highest level. But in Freemasonary they divide it to several levels, saying it has different meaning depending how high a level you rise to in the Freemasonary Order. The lower levels of the many Porch Masons these are the Esoteric Masons that are given the teachings of the body of secret knowledge of the profane, and so they believe they are in the know, but they are only given information that means Geometry, and God. Then at the next higher level they tell them that it means Gnosis, meaning intuitive apprehension of Spiritual truths, an Esoteric form of mystical knowledge, then at the higher levels that are above the thirty two degree of Masionary, at the Illuminated level they are talt, the truth of of the real reality of the meaning of the G in the Masonic symbol, that it stands for the Generative Principle, the Eighth Principle that encompasses all of the other Seven Principles of the fundamentals of Manifested Life in the Animated Form of Geomancy. The G of Generative Principle also stands for Genesis, meaning Creation. But in Esoteric Freemasonary at the absolute highest levels the G stands for the most important Principle of all, the Eighth Generative Principle of Life, the Principle of Geomancy, and the Principle of Creation. The meaning of the Generative Principle means to Create, which comes from the Latin word Generative, with the verb Genere meaning to Create, because we Create through the Generative Principle. So how does this Generative Principle work, it works on the Love energy intention directed at what we care about enough, to put our Will Life Force Energy behind it in Mental Projection, to manifest in physical reality. So we come back then to the heart, the mind, and gut, the gut is our Will, and our Courage of action, of the Masculine Principle, this is what gets things achieved in the physical realm. So what we Love and Care enough to put our Will behind, that's driven by the Love of Caring, from the Heart, the Generator that is the pump that drives the Will, so what we actually Love and Care about, by putting our Will behind it, is ultimately what gets manifested into

Creation, into our encompassing environment, into our Physical World. We can perceive the World is the way that it is because humanity has been steered in this direction by the Brotherhood of the Snakes, with misdirections of the truth of reality relating to the Eight Principles of Life, of Geomancy, of Creation. Thus the Worldwide citizens have been worn down and don't vibrate Love of Caring as much, but they want change and for things to be different, but their action never matches, because it is normally inactions that prevent us from the change we desire. It becomes action preventing action, and this is exactly what the New Age Ideology is designed to do by the Occultists, because they want World citizens to be inactive, because the Dark Occultists know that the thing that is ultimately generating our reality is behaviour. So action is what is generating the reality that gets generated through what we Love and Care about, because our Love and Caring and our Desires, then become our actions, or inactions if not enough attention of focused Mental Energy is directionally and Intentenally exerted, on the desired manifested out come, which is what is happening with many people Worldwide, they want change, but their actions, their behaviors stay the same, so no change can manifest, under the Eight Principles of the fundamental Laws of Nature. So humanity has to get out of the Monkey Mind, get out of the negative cycles of polarity in Maya and take responsibility, to control our Minds, our thoughts, and with Morality, utilise all aspects of the Eight Principles and fundamental Laws of Geomancy, the Sacred Laws of the Creation, of Nature, of Life.

CHAPTER TWO

The Great Work
An Introduction To The Human Eternal Light Body

The Great Work, of truth, freedom and love, is the work of awakening the masses to the true nature of the Ego Mind, to create an an environment to encourage all Worldwide citizens to use their Critical Thinking Mind and to have courage to face their own inner dark shade of self the negative of our selfs, and to practice the Natural Law of positive Expressions, understanding that what we use to create that of expressions of Generative Polarity, in the positive it is Consciousness from Love, and in the negative it is UnConsciousness from

Fear, then in the expression of Initiating expressions of how it starts, in the positive it is acceptance of Truth of Knowledge, and in the negative it is Ignorance and the refusal of Truth, then in the expression of Internal expression of whats happening inside us, in the positive it is Internal Monarchy of Sovereignty, and in the negative it is Internal Anarchy causing Confusion, then in the expression of whats happening in our environment in our Society, in the positive its Freedom of External Anarchy, and in the negative it is Control of External Monarchy, then in the expression of Manifestation the result we create, in the positive it is Order and all manifested is Good, and in the negative it is Chaos which manifests Evil.

The truth is that the Law of Freedom is known, that freedom and morality are directly proportional, and as morality increases, so does freedom increase. And as morality declines, so does freedom decrease. So if humanity instead practices Love, coming from their Heart-Mind with

Love in their manifestations, then humanity will then experience and know, and be in a State of Freedom, by accessing higher levels of Vibrational Consciousness. The problems is the masses of which many are unaware that they are in a Mindset of Defacto Satanism, which will lead them down the path of absolute domination with complete enslavement.

This is why we must share our ancient knowledge with others of the Mind, of the Ego, of Source, of Universal history of the Angelic Seed Wars, of DNA Biotechnology, of Spirit, of Nature, of Energy, of the Eternal, of Consciousness, of Physics and Psychology of the Mechanics and Mechanisms of Life and the Creation. Then we can evolve Individually and Collectively as planned by our Creators from Source the Yanas Ascended Masters, that designed us to evolve into Embodied Eternal Angelic Human Light beings, to evolve as a Collective Human Eternal race to take control of our Destiny as a Species. We must pass knowledge to all Worldwide citizens about their Schematic Blueprint within their DNA, that informs the Luminous Energy Field the Software to upgrade and then manifest and grow a new body via the Hardware the DNA, to grow a new Eternal Human Light Body, but to attain this one must overcome the negative polarity of our Individual Ego's.

Namaste I recognize the Eternal Immortal Soul within each of you, the human Spirit, the Divine Spark within, we are beings of Peace of Light and Love and Pro-Life. Namaste to all, we have watched the World around in chaos, we have been watching the propaganda Worldwide Media machine and Worldwide Free Press push narratives and agendas and talk on Polilitics, Religion, War, and the Fallen Angels desendants Royal Elite Globalist Cabal Cult agendas of Worldwide Genocide of all Nations, Religions and Citizens of Planet Gaia. We don't see or hear of

Politicians or Religious Leaders tell citizens of Earth the truth, so I wish to share an important message at this time in the now in the present moment.

I hope you take this information on board and share with your fellow man and woman to all citizens of Earth, for it is time for leaders to speak truth and warn citizens of the Importance of this Ancient Knowledge and Wisdom I am going to share as it was to me, through decades of critical research and thinking. Many on Earth are aware but many are not, that negative forces have waged Psychological Warfare upon you the Whole of your Lifes, many World citizens are waking up Consciously, from their programming and indoctrination and brainwashing, there has been a continuum of attacks manifesting as a War on your Minds, on your Eternal Consciousness, your Spirit.

Its time World Leaders told you the truth of the Political and Religious Dogma that's been fabricated for control of

World citizens and their Minds, so I impart this Ancient Knowledge for the well being of the Whole race the Whole of Human Civilization for all of Humanity, for the future are the children's children's children, because we elders must past knowledge and wisdom to the next generations, its our Eternal duty, for the Souls Spiritual growth and path to Enlightenment. All religions on Earth are made up Dogma, a Principle or set of Principles laid down by an Authority as incontrovertibly true. Now Spiritual practices to include Shamanism which is the Original Spiritual practice of the Universe, tell us in scripture or oral traditions, to have Love in our Hearts, Honor and to Respect Ourselfs and our Neighbours and you shall find the Light and enter the Kingdom of Heaven.

What this actually means, you shall find the Light and enter the Kingdom of Heaven is – Our DNA flashes a 100Hz a second, our DNA flashes light a hundred times a second, every cell of your body is flashing light, vibrating at frequency, and has a Luminous Energy Field around the Human Avatar, the Human biological body.

So World citizens you have a Luminous Energy Field around your Avatar, that envelopes your biological physical body, that is a foot above your head, a foot below your feet and stretches outwards as far as your arms stretch out, the Luminous Energy Field that envelopes your physical body, organises the body for example, if you have a glass table top and you place metal iron filings on the glass top and place a magnet underneath, the metal filings are attracted to the magnet and create form, a shape connected together to create one iron file body.

The Luminous Energy Field is the Software that informs the Hardware the DNA to grow the Human biological body, you are not the Mind or Body, you are Eternal Ultra Violet Energetic Consciousness, weighing Twenty One grams.

The Hardware DNA manifactures the physical body, and when we download the latest version of the Software, by reaching into the future and stepping into who we are becoming and receiving the instructions that will reprogramme our DNA, that helps us to create new bodies that age differently, die differently and heal differently.

To do this we have to raise our bodies vibration, coming from the heart, with love in our hearts and eating a high vibrational vegetarian diet, and with practices of meditation, prayer and other ancient disiplines like yoga, tai chi, qigong, martial arts, reki and other energy disciplines.

So when scripture says you will find the light, it means you can open and access your Eternal Light Body, stop the cycles of Life and Death, stopping your Karmatic cycles of Reincarnation. This will bring you back to your true nature of an Eternal Immortal Interdimensional Light being of Conscious Energy, no longer separated from the Universe, you are able to travel in the Hyper-Dimensional Matrix of all dimensions and realities, you are then living being fully embodied in a 5th dimensional Earth reality, but able to leave your body at will or travel with your body in a sixty foot field of light by travelling through the portholes Sun to Sun, Solar System to Solar System, Galaxy to Galaxy, or you can just teleport when you understand you are powdered light beyond the perception of light waves.

So we are Immortal Interdimensional Light beings of Divine Conscious Energy, we flash DNA to create different looking bodies, different species and races, and in the now different human bodies, to have different human experiences, different races, religions and live in different cultures and societies, to grow Spiritually and pay past Karma off from past Incarnations.

The Universe is One photon, One particle of Light refracting down to Galaxies and Solar Systems and Planets and biological

Life, so the Universe and our physical bodies are flashing light at different frequencies of vibrations at different densities. We are all one family of Light in the Creation, the Brahman, the Whole.

My advice is to study the Nine Rites of Initiation of the MUNAY-KI RITES, to be able to learn about your Light Body and how to grow it Consciously, with fire ceremonies along with diet, mediation, yoga and other energy and light disiplines and martial arts studies. Also research Dr Alberto Villoldo a medical anthropologist who has had 25 years apprenticeship with the Laki people high in the Andes and Amazon rainforests.

This Ancient Knowledge has been hidden and supressed by the Elite Cult, but our Ancestors the Keepers of past Wisdom and Knowledge handed them down by sound of word in oral traditions, and in hieroglyph form, in secret, or incomprehensible symbols and writings, by different cultures and races to the next generations to pass down the knowledge for all to benefit. That is why the Elite Cult wiped out and exterminated the tribal and native peoples of Earth, as they could teach you about Spirit, Energy, Plant Medicines and Healing, so they genocided many races of tribes and cultures, so they could not pass this knowledge on, because they want you controlled, to be their slave on Earth, and not have access to the Multiverse, the Hyper-Dimensional Matrix of Creation and to stop you accessing your Eternal Light Body via your DNA.

So we reside and live in a physical body and Universe made of flashing vibrating light in a Holographical Universe of Light, we are all one family of Light in the Creation. Ancient knowledge and Spiritual practices teach us we are Spirit, to live by way and in harmony with nature, never take more than needed for Eternal balance.

Your Luminous Energy Field can be accessed through your DNA, the part of the DNA the main stream science call

JUNK DNA but it is not, it's a lie, there is a Schematic Blueprint within the non-junk DNA to grow a Luminous Light Body, allowing you to stop the cycles of life and death and evolve from Homo-Sapian to Homo-Luminous, allowing you to ascend, meaning being in your body fully but also able to access all dimensions of reality in this Universe and the Multiverses, accessing the Hyper-Dimensional Matrix of Life, of Existence.

The dark forces on Earth that are moving against humanity on many levels at this moment in time, but my concern is for World citizens and most important is the children for they are the future of the race, the future of the Species of Human that we are. Right now many World citizens are now aware of the multi mass child and adult murder and maimer via Biological Virus Weapons, from Bill and Miranda Gates Foundation and their accomplices, and there Eugenics agendas from the same Elite Cult, they have shown their hand, members in the Blood

Cult, pushing there Synthetic made Biological Vaccine Weapons Program on Worldwide citizens and their children, that's child abuse in the first degree, to depopulate and sterilize and poison World citizens and Humanites children.

Now the Secret Truth on the Spiritual level of understanding is that they are trying to stop you opening your Light Body, to stop you opening your Luminous Energy Fields and stop you from ascending and evolving to Homo-Luminous.

They are with these Biological Weapon Vaccines trying to damage your RNA the building blocks of your DNA, so you can not access the Blueprint in your DNA with the Informational Plans and design of the Schematic of your Eternal Immortal Light Body.

The True negative Intent behind these Biological Weapon Vaccines, is to stop you and your children from opening your Light Bodies, Ascending and travelling in the Hyper-Dimensional Matrix, made up of all dimensions and densities of reality. So it is imperative for World citizens to not, I say again to not put Biological Weapon Vaccines in yourself and your childrens bodies, that alter your RNA the building blocks of your DNA.

Within your DNA are the instructions of a Blueprint to grow a new body that lives differently, dies differently and heals differently. The Blueprint of a Homo-Luminous Body of Light, once accessed through a diet of plants, high vibrational and through meditation, prayer and many ancient practices and disiplines and through ceremonies.

You grow the Luminous Light Body Consciously with your Mind the tool of the Avatar, silence and stillness is part of the key and diet to access your Kundalini Energy Systems, then you will be able to stand in your Eternal Power and you will start to experience your gifts and strengths.

I wish you all well in your journey of accessing your Light Bodies on the path of Ascension, blessings to all of humanity and the children the future of the human race, remember we are One, United in the Oneness of all that be in Creation, we are in Service to the Oneness to all Sentient beings, blessings Namaste LoveLifeLee.

The Creator of Light that's you and me, gave us Free Will, by Divine decree, no Government, Corporation, Religion, Elite Extraterrestrial blood Cult, no ethenic group has the right to tell you how to live on Earth, so long as you follow the Eight Principles od Natural Law and Universal Law, live in Peace, Love thy neighbour, be treated as you wish to be treated, logic and common sense really.
Namaste I wish all beings in Creation and on Earth to have inner peace to project outer peace, to attain enlightenment to not suffer with sorrow to be lead from mortality to immortality, to see the illusion that surrounds them, I wish you all Consciousness, to raise your embodied Avatar biological bodies Vibration and for you to Ascend and access and travel the Creation, the Cosmos in its entirety,

for you and me we be Angels, do you see, Light beings, Interdimensional, Eternal maninfesting from Divine Ultra Violet Energetic Consciousness, blessings on your Earth walk of Life and on your journey home to the kingdom of light, via Ascension, Namaste LoveLifeLee.

Activating the Chakra Energy System to Awaken our Kundalini Life Force Energy to Activate our Pineal Gland our Third Eye To Access Our Eternal Light Body

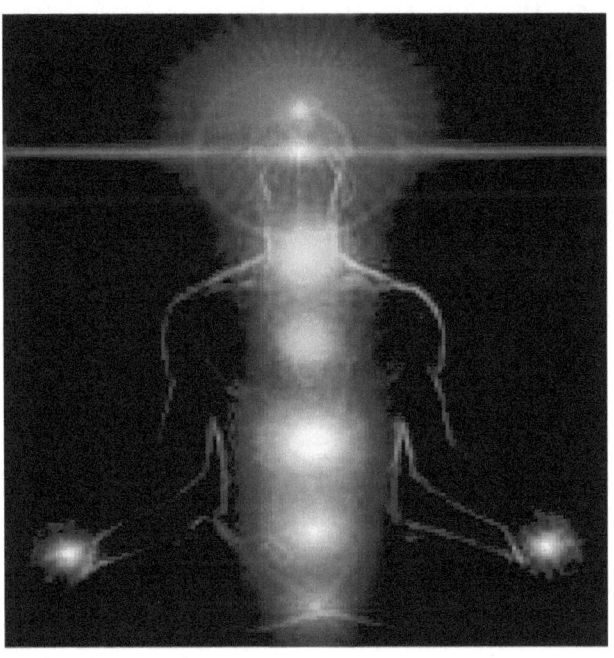

CHAPTER THREE

Part 1

An Introduction To Meditation

Meditation comes from Principles from the Indian Vedic Scripture and practices, it is also from the Tibetian Scriptures and practices, and from many different Tribal Cultures on Planet Gaia our Mother Earth also known as Pachamama.

Meditation is a Holistic practice from Holistic traditions from the Eastern and Western practices, this is characterized by the belief that the parts of something are intimately interconnected and explicable only by reference to the Whole.

This meditation knowledge is inspiring

and full of ancient ways, traditions of meditation for the well being, health, upliftment and for a rise in Consciousness, which will allow access to the Zero Point Energy Field of the Universe and Creation.

Meditation will bring you inner peace, stillness, clarity, and allow you to control the mind by controlling the emotional body, controlling the emotions, you will start to clearly see you are not the Body or Mind, that we reside in these manifested Human Avatars, but that at the core we are Eternal Light beings, we are Divine Energy beings from the Immortal realm outside of time and space, where the kingom of Light is the Kingdom of Heaven.

Meditation is the key to peaceful manifestations, then your inner peaceful thoughts will manifest outwards into vibratory words and actions, creating your physical reality of your choosing.

Through stillness of the mind with the accompaniment of breath work and ancient breath practices, you will create space to have clarity, with clarity you will see the mind is just a tool of the human avatar, the human biological body in which we manifest.

We manifest through the Luminous Energy Field that is around our bodies, it encompasses us, the Luminous Energy Field is the Software that informs the Hardware the DNA to grow the Avatar the biological human body, the Luminous Energy Field is a foot below your feet, a foot above your head and as wide as your arms stretch outwards.

Meditation combined with breath work will allow your energy flow systems (your Chakra Systems and m Meridian Energy flow Systems) to operate at a higher optimal rate, combined with the Ancient practices like Yoga, Martial Arts, Tai Chi, Qi Gong or and Healing Energy practices like Reiki Energy healing, Sekhmet Energy healing, and with Shamanic practices and Shamanic ceremonies, you will raise your bodies Vibrational frequencies and in turn raise your Consciousness, which will allow access to the Zero Point Energy Field of Creation allowing access to the Hyper-Dimensional Templar Light Time Matrix of the Whole of the Creation, the Brahman, the Whole.

To start Meditation find a space that is quiet and tranquil with no distractions, light incense or you can sage the space you find your self in for this meditation practice, also I recommend when starting to light a candle, that you can focus on and then see in the Minds eye, until you will step beyond it and see it in your Minds eye with clear vision, as in time with practice, you will control your thoughts like clouds floating past the eye of the Mind, and you will see them, the thoughts for what they are and will be able to choose if you act on them or not, for the Monkey Mind can play tricks on you, via the emotional body, until you can control your emotions which leads to vibatory spoken words and actions one may not of actually wanted to express, silence and breath the key to attain clarity, with clarity one controls the thoughts and then controlling your manifestations and that of your manifested reality that surrounds and encompasses you.

Meditation is a practice for all, for every Soul on the Planet, and is a practice you can learn on your own, by your self for it is about looking within, to create an inner peace.

So Meditation is a journey of Self discovery, it is a Personal journey within, you can go to a meditation class with a teacher to get the basics, or learn by your self.

Meditations benefits you will see rather quickly, almost immediately you will feel calmer, more focused and centred feeling much more grounded. You will after a little practice feel a deep sense of an instinctive harmony within and with the World around you, you will get a stronger deeper connection with your inner self and you will connect to your senses and perceive more around you, you will access more of your intuition allowing you have the ability to understand things more instinctively with out the need for Conscious reasoning.

Like any thing it can take time to learn the practice of Meditation, don't allow yourself to become frustrated, their can be pitfalls along the ways or occasions that seem that the practice of Meditation is being frustratingly slow. Keep positive don't lose heart.

Meditation should not ever be the cause of upset via frustration, you should not feel discomfort. As this will not be beneficial, take breath and come back to the meditation practice later that day or the next day.

Remember Meditation is the practice of harnessing the control of the Mind, control of thoughts, then we are able to control the Eternal Mental Chi Energy that is at the Core of our Eternal being.

When we practice Meditation by adapting and drawing upon these ancient traditions and practices, it will become intuitive and a natural way of being in our daily lifes, controlling our manifestations then controlling our enveloped reality, remember Meditation practices are an exciting exploration inwards of your own self.

So the truth known is that we are Interdimensional Light beings Vibrating at frequency in a manifested form, so we are not the Human Avatar, biological body and we are not the Mind.

So we need to Meditate, then this true reality of what we are as manifested human beings and the energy forces behind the physical form that of Spirit will be seen, and also the different realities of Worlds, Solar Systems, Galaxies and Universes of different dimensions.

To be fit in Mind Body and Spirit and to have a healthy Avatar and to function as a healthy human being to be at our peak at our fullest potential, we must look within and learn about our Soul and protect the Inner self, for the outer distractions are all around in material forms, designed for you to be disconnected from within, bringing disharmony a lack of connection to the Inner Self the Soul, and Creates Unease causing disease of the Mind and Body, manifesting as Mental Illnesses and Physical Illness in the Body by way of mutated cells.

So we must Create time and space to spend and give to our Inner selfs, we must not allow the outer needs to Govern us in our Minds and Bodies, we need to listen to the Inner Self and not ignore that Intuitional Selfs advice, whether it be to slow down, take a rest or at a particular moment our health will suffer, and our ability to with stand high pressure situations and stressfull moments in Life will be Weakened.

So Meditation is an Ancient practice that is by design able to be an effective way to ensure that we are not neglecting our Inner Selfs, our Inner Voice, our Inner Intuition, then we will no longer fail to take care of our Inner Selfs properly, as the most important aspect of our well being is to look after and control in all aspects of the Mind, our Psychological State, then we can achieve all personal effectiveness in all aspects of our Lifes.

So this goal can be achieved with starting off with five minutes a day and build it up as time goes by, up to an hour a day may be you will feel comfortable with two half hour sessions one in the morning and one in the evening.

There is no need to go into hours of Contemplation, then by doing smaller amounts of time in each Meditation session gradually, you will begin to understand the Body and Mind relationship, and in that process you will have a discovery of a new dimension in your Life.

Meditation for twenty minutes naturally rejuvenates the body and gives a huge boost to your Immune System, Meditation allows us to heal deep within Ourselves that we were Unaware even needed healing, as all the distractions of modern Life with screens, flashing light, waves of sound frequencies and bad food, distract Us from Within.

So Meditation is about the understanding and development of the Meditation practices and space not the amount of time you spend in each session, that will come naturally over months and years of practice, at my peak it was up to two hours a day, then I was happy with two one hour sessions and when busy two half hour sessions one in morning one in the evening, which allowed my Mind to be calm and not racing, and then falling asleep quicker and put in a deeper State of Sleep for a deeper level of healing to occur in the physical body.

Part 2

Realizing The Connections Of The Body & Mind

To live a prosperous life which is harmonious and nourished in balance their must be a mutual relationship of dependency between the body and the mind, they must work together in Unison as One not being isolated from one another, they must be Connected and Unified.

We must learn to understand about the way we feel and think of ourselves has a direct influence on matter on our biological system, on our Avatar our Human bodies, and having a healthy body creates a healthy Mind and the opposite, a healthy Mind creates a healthy Body, they must work as One.

Look its simple really with negative thoughts from a negative state of mind, you will produce a negative outcome in your physical reality, we have been programmed and indoctrinated by our families, teachers, societies controlled belief systems, by negative forces in the background who want to rule the human race. When you have positive thoughts from a positive Mindset, your manifested physical reality that surrounds you will change and you will attract only the positive good things you wish to manifest into being, into your physical life, then you will be able to attain yout highest potential not only as a human being but accessing yout Light Body via your DNA, then able to being present in your bodies fully, and enlightened able to access the Universe and other dimensions, no longer having to leave the physical body via the death construct of the Human Mind, created to have a meaning for the Existance of Life, to have a meaning of the Purpose of Life.

With meditation we can change the quality of our lives through interpretation and from exploration of the Inner Self, and our relationships to our bodies, minds and our manifested realities, we then will start to see the symbiotic relationship between the Body and Mind, we start to see the connections, actions and reactions, via the emotional body, the emotional thoughts that cause the actions we act on in the form of vibrational words or physical actions.

Then we start to access the UnConscious Mind, and we can see how the Conscious and UnConscious Mind interconnect and manifest, some times what we wish for, other times not what we wish for, we see they are patterns, cycles to be broken to move away from the programming, indoctrination and brain washing that we picked up from family, teachers and societies programmed belief systems. We brake away beyond the false narrative created to control Society, to control the Whole Human Civilization, orchestrated by a few from the Fallen Angels bloodlines.

We can start to understand thoughts through meditation and start to see the motivations, the Universe is a mandelbhrot set, it's a refractual of its self on a continuum in manifested physical reality and in a Co-Collective Consciousness. So the true reality in Creation is in pictorial form, born of images, when we meditate they come to us in the Minds eye as if appearing as dreams, these are manifested by the UnConscious Mind and were created by the energies of the UnConscious Mind.

These dream like pictorial form of symbols and images and pattern forms of three dimensional geometry that we see in meditation have significance and are symbolic in nature, not all ways to be taken as quite literal in manner or sense or as exactly as it is. You will be able with Meditation practice to interact in your Minds eye and explore these images and symbols, this will then allow you interact with the creative process and move them from your UnConscious Mind to your Conscious Mind, then you start to decode the puzzle of the symbol or images, a piece of information in light form from all spectrums and densities of light. This will then allow you to understand and reveal their true meanings and messages.

It is important when meditating to be aware of what is happening inside you, your Inner Self and also to be aware of your outer Ego Self, the character you play role for this human experience, and what is actually happening in your life at the time, then you will see the significance of the coincidences and see there is a purpose and meaning to a particular personal situation, event, or connections with others in your immediate circle of family, friends and work associates.

Any chance meetings in life are not a

coincidence they are manifested from the UnConscious Mind or another example is when you think you should call a particular person and that person contacts you, and some times at a rapid pace of manifestation. You are actually both connected to the Co-Creative human Consciousness Energy Field , also connected to the what as known as the ether, so be wary and careful even cautious with your thoughts, one must control the Monkey Mind that goes off on its own tangent, meaning to take you on a completely different line of thought. The tangent the UnConscious energy of the Mind goes back to is of thoughts in its old programming cycles, until you can through Meditation you can control the mind, then controlling the emotions, thus controlling your actions, most importantly for the Whole Human Civilization is to control all manifestions, to create a peaceful, abundant reality for us all to Co-Exist in a World of wonder built from love and light, creating a World of beauty, of amazement that is magical in nature, and for us all to be connected as One manifesting and Co-Creating as One Collective.

Part 3

Why Meditate
What Is Meditation

There are many reasons many Souls turn to Meditation, a whole host of different varieties of lifes tough challenges, situations and experiences. In this hectic busy Society today more people are dealing with stress, with high pressure to survive and to provide, in stressful enviroments with harmful technologies with dangerous frequencies that distort your geometric biological cell structure that are in your work places and in your homes.

People are drawn to Meditation to eliminate unnecessary stress and the tension they hold and carry in the body and in their lives and these people wish to learn to relax on a deep level, when actually practicing Meditation, when you come out of the Medative State you will be refreshed and return with that Inner knowing after connecting to your Inner Self, your Eternal Spirit, and you can then have clear decise perspectives, with a positive out come with situations in your daily life, all you have to do is make time and create the space to practice Meditation, with a daily set time and length of time and routine, breaking bad old cycles and bringing in new positive affirmations and manifestations will be achieved with Meditation.

Meditation is salvation from Self, to be in a state of being saved or protected from harm or a dire situation ones UnConscious Mind has created, so Meditation is salvation, it is the deliverance of the Soul from Sin and consequences from the UnConscious Mind that we were not in control of via our emotional and Psychological States, we must manifest at the level of Spirit from the Eternal Spirit body not from the three other bodies below the Psychological body or the Emotional body or the Physical body.

When you see the Monkey Mind the UnConscious Mind and its continuum of endless thoughts many on a repetative cycle of programming, all of the time you are awake and when you are on your own, you see that your Mind is never really focused on one particular thought of a job or task to be done, it does not really focus on a particular activity, these thoughts flip flop and move in all directions, and most of the time the UnConscious Mind is firing Chi thought Energy in an unorchestrated, unarranged of the cuff in the moment nonrepetitive pattern.

These thoughts from the UnConscious Mind are controlled through Meditation, these thoughts come from the emotional body, from the emotional responses and are unconstructive, they come from the emotional States we have through fear, anxiety and stress, we need to all ways depress with Meditation, then the silence and breath control will be bringing you Inner peace and stillness this then brings clarity. Then a Inner knowing that you can control your Mind, your thoughts, your emotions and then your actions and reactions to circumstances and situations that occur in Life, and the Interactions with other Eternal Souls, that's us, for we truly are Eternal Immortal Interdimensional Light beings of Ultra Violet Divine Energetic Consciousness, we are Spirit in Nature.

Meditation is the key to accessing the m Meridian Energy Systems and the Chakra Energy Systems via your Consciousness, this then with diet and other Ancient Chi Energy practices we spoke on earlier in the book, will give you access to your Eternal Light Body, via Conscious access of your own DNA, to grow the Light Body, and with fire ceremonies, it will manifest into being and you will become an Illuminated Angelic Human being of

Light, Ascend and Transcend all dimensions in the Hyper-Dimensional Templar Light Time Matrix of Creation. Meditation is the tool to connect our Bodies and Minds, to be in touch with the Inner Self, we can then start to comprehend the desires and motivations of the UnConscious Mind, this allows us see the negative thought and the negative old cycles and we can then delete those old emotional feelings that do not serve us but harm us, knock us out of balance in our Chi Energy flow Systems, so then we can make the changes for the better once we see that our Inner Selfs were operating from the negative energetic forces of the UnConscious thoughts the UnConscious Mind.

The Meditation posture, the correct position is called the lotus position with the spine vertical, straight and the legs crossed folded inwards and the arms either resting on your knees with the thumb and fore fingers connected or with the arms tucked into the naval with the hands together with the fingers interlocking and thumbs touching, this creates a physical posture that allows energy to flow correctly around the body, through the Meridian Energy System and then through the Chakra System.

If you are disabled or elderly and unable to sit cross legged on the floor on a cushion or on a couch, you can just sit in a chair with the spine upright, straight and arms and hands interlocking, with your feet on the floor but if possible have your feet touching for the energy to flow in a circuit.

The physical and practical benefits of Meditation are World renowned and well recognized Globally, with good correct posture and breath control you will encourage the body to lose tension and to relax, this will enable the body to function at a higher level, to become more efficient, your energy levels will go up, your creativity will flourish. Then the disease of the body will slowly start to dissipate, to dissolve to fall away. This then will reveil that of some of your Eternal Soul characteristics, you will slowly get to know your Spirit essence, a clear relationship of the Body and Mind, and an understanding of who you truly are as an Eternal Light being, as a Cosmic Angelic Guardian of the Creation.

When you have a routine of Meditation in place daily you will see the benefits the rewards with a little time and space created, you will be in a more tranquil state much more relaxed in your daily routine and life, you find you have access to deeper levels of the mind of the psyche and a clearer perspective of life your body, mind, emotional wel being, your manifestation abilities will rise with stillness and concentration you will have Clarity, challenges and problems will no longer be large obstacles, but a small stepping stone to cross, then with this raised Consciousness we can see past the illusion of the false reality created by the Fallen Angel bloodlines, and then we can see past the Universes make up of the other illusion that we reside in, that is that we are in a University of Holographic VibrationalLlight. On the deeper levels then we can become aware what it truly means to be an Eternal Light being in the manifested form of a Human being, as we start to perceive all Life is Interconnected, it is One fabric of Light woven in time and space, on an ever lasting continuum, its just Divine, magical in Nature, awesome love it.

Part 4

Meditation With A Candle

Meditation with a candle was how I first started sixteen years ago, the candle is a good way to learn to focus to start in Meditation sessions.
So calm the mind sit in the lotus position if you are physically able to, use a cushion to rise your bum and it will be much more comfortable, if not sit in chair make sure your hands and fingers inter lock, if resting at the naval, if in lotus position if hands separate make sure fore finger and thumb linked for energy flow.

So light a candle and place in line of eye sight, focus on the candle, afrer taking a few deep breaths to oxygenate the blood, breath evenly but slighty deeper than normally, tell yourself and communicate to the cells of your body asking it to relax, do this a few times, then start to focus on the candle flame, see the flame enter your third eye, your eyes closed, flame in pictorial form in the Minds eye, and become One with the flame, see no seperatness you fuse as One, it becomes a part of your being. This is a good way to learn to focus the third eye and start visualization, ending the Meditation become aware of your breath again, and breathe slightly deeper for a few minutes, then you can open your eyes, you should feel refreshed, if you Meditated with spine straight for twenty minutes you boosted your Immune System, so be Mindful to stay calm through out your day always come back to the breath if stressed, or have any anxiety.

Unwind Loosen Relax The Body

So enter a relaxed state, begin your Meditation, by sitting in the correct position spine up right straight, or if unable to do this lie on your back in a comfortable position, beathe deeply then easily and freely. Start by concentrating, by focusing on each part of the body relaxing each part in turn, I always start at my feet then ankles, lower legs, then upper legs, the pelvis reigon, then lower body the stomach area the lower torso, upper torso the chest, I do my arms, then sholders, neck, my heart then my face, my eyes, most important say several times, I relax my Mind, ending with my Mind is completely relaxed.
Imagine you are feeling lighter, say I am lighter the weight of all the tension and stress have left my body, then say the lighter I feel the deeper relaxed I become, again take some deep breaths then freely breath and open your eyes, you will be amazed that such simple process will take

the stress disease away an you should feel rejuvenated.

In this Meditation process of relaxing all of the body, after a time you can do deeper relaxed Meditation healings, by going inside the body focus on the part its function and place your Mind, your Consciousness to that particular part of the body, I do my muscles, tendons, blood vessels, bones, imagining down to the micro level of bone marrow and the structural make up of the bone, my liver, kidneys, I visualize the blood flowing freely and so on, it is very powerful when you learn to place your Consciousness to each part of the body you are healing, see your Consciousness as Ultra Violet healing light as this is the make up of your Chi Consciousness Energy.

Part 5

Meditation & The Breath

The breath effects our mental and physical States, many people are not Conscious of this fact, it is cruial that we observe the breath in Meditation and become One, become symbiotic observing the way we breathe, for this is how to control the emotions, the Psyche the Monkey Mind. So take a minute or two to breathe filling the lungs as a steady breath creates a calming effect and stills the Mind for Clarity to come through that will then allow your intuition to flow freely and to make decisions from your first brain the stomach the gut. The deep breaths will allow the expulsion of waste gases to leave the body and reoxygenate the blood and then in turn the body.

We learn that Meditation is a focusing on the breath and we learn to regulate the breath, to control all systems of the Mind and in turn the Body systems, we then can develop over time to control the body via breath, then with focus on Mind we can control the emotional body, then control our action and reactions, controlling our behaviours, this leads to a much better higher quality of Life.

The correct posture for Meditation and the correct breathing is fundimentally linked, when Meditating always lose the tension to start, your diaphragm and lungs need to be able to move freely, this is why the correct postion is paramount, because when you get to deep states of Meditation, you no longer breathe from your upper chest but you breathe from deep in the diaphragm as this is the most effective way of breath control to enter deep States of Meditation.

Before starting contemplation the process of breathing and you realize no breath, no life your existance depends on it, then you will realize the importance it plays in your life for health and well being and to have peaceful Mind, and so you can manifest your physical reality that surrounds you, again the importance no breath, no Life.

One must learn to have Contemplation of our environment, the elemental energy of air and our connection, the relationship that we have, we become One, symbiotic we learn the importance of every exhalation and inhalation as breathing is a Meditation in it's Self.

Part 6

The Development Of Your Focus

The key is to centre ones self before Meditation, to focus our Mind and to still the body, then we can enter a State of Concentration, then we can absorb the stillness with Clarity and start to perceive the images in pictural form, that you will access in deep States of Meditation, this is you accessing the Creation via the mandelbhrot set of fractals the true reality of the Cosmos, in its vibatory light forms of different densties of realities. These images in pictural form then can be transferred from the UnConscious Mind to the Conscious Mind to be deciphered, these messages will help us in our lives and in the understanding of this Universe the Holographical University for Souls to manifest into to experience and grow Spiritually, and to start to perceive and understand Creation, in all its Vibatory forms, and the energies behind Life behind Creation.

So before Meditation we must leave all personal preconseptions behind and all preoccupations we have in our daily lives, then our Attention can focus and rest in your Awareness, so one must focus their Chi Energetic Consciousness by channelling all your Mental energy, on the specific part of the body if healing and going inside the Body or Mind, or focusing on any images coming in to your third eye. Eventually you will find your thought will become one, in the moment in the present, when channelled and directed to a part of body or when focused on an in coming image.

At first when starting Meditation you will have distractions from time to time while leaning to control the Monkey Mind, and allow yourself to see thoughts in your Minds eye as clouds floating past and you can choose to act on the thought or not depending on whether it serves you in your Life, but with practice and dedication, especially after you feel, see and experience the benefits and access to the Creation, over time your concentration levels will increase and become Powerful, after a while you will see the enriching benefits and experiences you gain like Law of Attraction, manifesting what you wish in your Life and over time your manifestation abilities will increase at a rapid pace.

We must achieve a sense of physical and mental balance by the development of focus and awareness, we realise that Meditation is a way of Life and to be blended into our daily Lifes in all moments, for we are Powerful manifesting Light being Angelic Goddesses and Gods, when we are pure in diet and in deep Meditation in every moment in the present, we use our manifesting Chi Energy instantaneously, with deep breath from the lower diaphragm we can focus and squeeze the area two inches below the naval, in the area between the abdomen down to the groin, this is called the Dantian an energy point in the body, there are three in total the others are in the heart area and the third eye area, by developing this practice you will over time find a physical and mental equilibrium.

So Meditation will a have a profound effect on you and your Life all with benefits, so long as you set the daily times and length of practice and make the space for Meditation, the rewards will blow your Mind, when the Illusions of reality and Self the Ego fall away. When you become focused on centering your self the balance of Body and Mind will naturally fall into place with focused Contemplation, we then will attract the positive blessings into our lives when we have learned to have a clear Mind, this comes in time after the dedication of regular practice.

Always remember there should be no

disease when Meditating some times you will feel discomfort at times when starting your Meditation practices, some times the tension is coming from the muscles, they can tighten this is caused as you are not relaxed enough or because your body is not yet comfortable in the new position, over time you will be able with some stretching before practice to stretch those muscles, tendons and tissues, so the new lotus position with your legs crossed tucked in and with the spine straight, will come with ease and the discomfort will fall away, no longer exist. You can also focus your Mind your Chi Energetic Ultra Violet Light Consciousness on the areas with tension, focusing on the blood pressure to decrease on the walls of the arteries, as there is to high a voltage in the raised blood pressure areas of tension. This will allow the blood to flow more freely and circulate at the right optimal rate, if you had any tingling sensations these should subside, drift away.

So one must learn to develop focus on Awareness, on our UnConscious thoughts and Conscious thoughts and place our Chi Energetic Consciousness, on the ones we wish to manifest and have that desired outcome.

Part 7

Centering Yourself

So important prerequisites for effective Meditation is to learn different exercises to develop a quiet and still mind with a firm body from the core. So while sitting in a comfortable position with your spine straight roll your shoulders back which will broaden your chest cavity, place your hands on your knees with hands palm face down when in lotus position, if sitting in chair your hands will be layed upon your thighs, focus your Mind on tension in the body and relax the muscles with your Intension and focus your chi energy in the tense area, always keep your breath steady with ease. Tap into your Inner strength of Self, if thoughts start drifting in, focus and blow them away and become more concentrated with your focus on your Chi Energy and the location you are placing it in the body or mind. You must learn to stabalize the UnConscious thought rhetoric of the mindless Monkey Mind, always come back to the focus on breath when uncontrolled thoughts enter the Mind. Another way to perceive things is the physical Awareness of the Avatar the body, by being present in the moment and feeling the weight of your body on your cushion or chair, to feel the heat of your body and the air that envolopes and encompasses it, this will allow you to consolidate your Awareness before you leave the Meditation State.

Part 8

Thought Watching

Associations come fron the involvement of the thinking Mind, we need to naturally allow our imagination and thoughts to expand and develop freely, with Meditation we need to monitor the various thoughts and feelings that arise spontaneously, so we must use both our ability to think and the imagination combined in the present moment.

We have to become aware and watch our thoughts and detach from them and start to observe them, the pictorial images and thoughts and allow then to flow naturally in and out of you, I see them as clouds drifting pass in my Minds eye then I observe them but I don't always engage with them with out judgement of them and with out influence, I become simply aware of them. I then start to notice the stillness and have the space to reflect on them and an Inner claming effect comes over me, you just have to have acceptance with the perspective of positive energy, in a positive light.

At times of distraction during Meditation, you will learn to come back to your centre and return to the focus of your Attention, then you can direct your Intention where you desire, you will become disciplined in your Medative practice, over time.

The idea is to be patient and non-judgemental but aware with a passive out look, you have to open yourself up to all possibilities, you can not assume anything or expect anything, if you get frustrated you are being judgemental on your self, don't let go lie down do a relaxed Internal Meditation Internally in the body and remove the tension.

Through out the day in daily routine of

life become aware of your thoughts, the feelings and thoughts that preoccupy you, identify them and Meditate on them in the next session. Many people fret and worry about things and situations in our lives that we have no control over, yet we allow this energy to effect us and change our State of Mind, our moods via our emotions. This leads to feelings of anger, fear, sadness, upset and hate these are negative thought forms creating negative out comes in our manifested realities that encompass us, so we must become strict observers of out day dreams, our thoughts and learn to identify the thought patterns that no longer serve us and remove them from the Software of our Consciousness. We then need to replace them with positive affirmations and thoughts that will manifest what we desire and truly wish for in our lives.

Part 9

Visulisation Of Images In The Eye Of The Mind

In Meditation the imagination enables us to delve more deeply and to see and focus more clearly on our inner most feelings and thoughts, when we are Meditating on an image or whether it be a sound of frequency we can see the effect it has on us via our close observations, you will then in time be able to conjure up and keep hold of these visions in the eye of the mind, it can take practice to retain these images for periods of time but will become easier just persevere.

Over time in Meditations you will be able to directly access the UnConscious Mind transfer the images of pictorial or vibrational sounds to your Conscious Mind and you will be able to allow with focus to expand and change these images in your Minds eye, and they will come to life even evolve. When in a Medative State and you are using your imagination you are building a bridge from the UnConscious Mind to the Conscious Mind, this new Conscious Awareness this connection allows access to a greater perspective and of a greater realization of our fullest potential, that of an awakened fully embodied Human being connected to Mind, Body and Soul, connected to the ether, we access our Light Bodies, which is the culmination of a twenty six thousand year manifesting cycle, we metamophis into our Eternal Angelic Rainbow Light Bodies, able to travel in the Whole of Creation, in the Hyper-Dimensional Templar Light Time Matrix of all realities and densities, the name that be prescribed is the Mandelbhrot fractal, that manifests as a continuum.

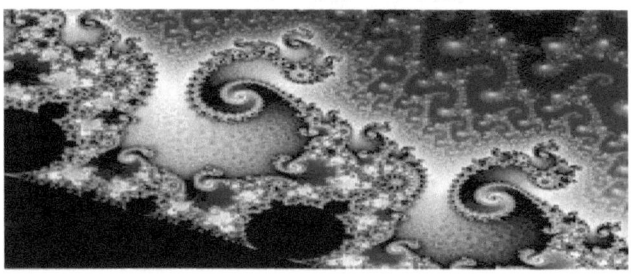

Part 10

The Way Of Life In Meditation

So now we know the basic Principles and techniques that we have familiarized our selfs through the practice of Meditation sessions, finding focus and attention on Awareness, we are equipped to go much more deeply into the Spiritual and Mental Wisdom and Knowledge in our resources, we will need to use them in a daily practice and in a present awake walking Meditation in every moment you will become truly present in your daily lives.

Meditation is concentration of the Inward Self, and focus of the Mind, but there is so much more to the Meditation experiences One can have, when you are Meditating daily, changes will happen and manifest in your physical life. You will choose the desired amount of commitment you wish to spend in the Medative State, the desired amount of time, as you have more connected and deciphered experiences, its natural you want to go back in and experience more of the pictorial images and vibrational sounds, and perceiving the next steps to take in Life with Clarity and a sense of Inner Peace.

So when we give our full attention to our Awareness of our feelings and thoughts that are taking place in the Body and Mind, we can start to see the concept of the well known phrase, Mindfulness. We need not to operate on impulses but control these old driving patterns of cycles that no longer serve us, like our attitude to Life to make sure we keep in a positive Mindset, and be in control of the urges that don't serve us like in our diets, we start to see all intake of food should be natural medicines like plants, herbs, nuts, barks,saps, seeds, roots, fruits and so on, we need these foods to power the Mind and Avatar the biological body, via the cells and at the micro level to feed the corners (the corners are the only solid on the Sacred Geometric structure of the building blocks of the Scaffolding of the Avatar the Human biological body), of the dodecahedrons with the amino acids from food, and to feed the corners of the tetrahedrons which are spinning in a hundred and twenty different patterns inside the dodecahedrons, the teterahedrons fed with proteins, the complexity and the simplicity of the biological life avatars and the holographical spaces we experience with the forces of electromagnetism, gravity and the strong and weak nuclear forces, Life is just magical in Nature.

If we are diligent with our learning from the Contemplation of our Inner Minds from Meditation, we learn to have no expectations, to be patient, have an open Mind and you will see that you manifest positive changes and outcomes into your Life.

Part 11

Having An Audience With Your Mind Becoming The Listener & Viewer

So lets be honest the Mind is constantly the joker, the trickster, it distracts us away from our Attention and uses many stratagies to do so, its trying to lead us astray it takes us down the wrong path and it deceives us, always being the joker using trickery and deception, these manifest as negative thoughts and feelings, most stem from a deep rooted fear, from old programming and indoctrination, these negative thoughts make it harder for us to succeed in our goals are dreams and ambitions, some times it seems the harder we try to be successful the more our thoughts can be obstructive.

Meditation allows us to stop this negative process to occur and to intervene and then keep you on the path to attain your Mental goal, the UnConscious Mind stems these obstructive and often intrucive thoughts, the UnConscious Mind operates and motivates our impulses, our instincts and our desires, if we do not make a commitment to engage with our UnConscious Minds, then we are not perceiving and listening to a most fundamental part of our Inner Core being. We also perceive that there is also positive and negative traits of the UnConscious Mind, the UnConscious Mind is like an onion so many layers, made up of many layers of each layer.

So we have many teachings and lessons learned through Meditation practices, we start to understand the mechanics of our UnConscious Mind, and we learn to make UnConscious thoughts tun into Conscious thoughts when we slowly and gradually get better acquainted with Inner works of the Mind. When you start to connect the

UnConscious mind and Conscious Mind as One you will have enhanced Wisdom and Knowledge, and your Self Awareness will blossom.

We must remember that the Mind when you meet it, and you begin to examine and dissect it, the encounters you have with it while in Meditation and after Meditation, are all different from other Souls, other people for we have and are experiencing many different realities all at the same time, while being connected whether you are Conscious of it or UnConscious of it, all happening in the now in the present, as One Creative and Co-Creative Collective Consciousness.

All Souls have many of the same needs and wishes and experience the wide range of emotions of love, joy, hate, desire, anger and fear, for under the skin we are all Light beings, race, culture, belief systems all fall away they are redundance and mostly obsolete, our characters our Egos Psychological make up from our past experiences, that diverge on different routes and go in many separate directions, in our history on our lifes path, in many different ways define our character.

So when starting out in Meditation try several ways of Meditation, if one way is not working for you try another until you are comfortable and able to concentrate on your breath, and then you will release tension then you will be able to relax the body, all this is acheieved via breath control and a stillness of the Mind.

Part 12

Becoming Aware Of Mindfullness

Mindfulness is coming to the realization on a very deep MultiConscious level, that the true value to life experience in manifested Avatar biological form is having a strong, rich Inner knowing the Spiritual way is to live Life present and to our fullest Potentials. We realize that the outward manifested materials distractions by design most of them, by dark forces with negative agendas, are not benefical and have negative effects upon us.

It is hard to concentrate in a Society which does not focus on Individual feelings, actions, thoughts and this can become increasingly difficult, in a goal driven Society Mentality, that surrounds and encompasses us with flashing bright lights and attractive Vibrational sounds, the Illusional distractions are shoved onto our Consciousness and onto our being and into our lives, as not to have the time and space to perceive with a Still Mind that we are Multidimensional Light beings in a Holographical University of Light.

Ancient philosophy and their traditions and practices offer an alternative way of being, and teach us the Nature of being, being present in every moment in the now, for the now is all we have in every eternal moment of experience via our manifested expression, and particular manifestations. So to find have and maintain Mindfulness we must have full Awareness of our thoughts, emotions, actions, and be aware of our sensations and movements. Then we are present when absorbed in the moment in the present in the now, so Meditation allows us to become fully alert which in its Self is a Mindful act of Intention.

As the Avatar the Human Body and Mind get older we seem or tend to forget the way our body, and breath feel to us and many are not even aware of their emotions and thoughts, as we go through life wondering along we are consumed and wrapped up in our thoughts, we are not alert our senses seem dulled and only half switched on. Not truly aware of our surroundings, to the sounds, smells, sights that are directed at at us on a continuum completely bombarding us, as we get older we seem to lose the skill of focus and don't give our experiences our full attention, we lose our concentration levels.

Meditation is when the Mind through breath is fully alert, we need to be fully alert and engaged in every aspect of our emotional, our physical, and our mental existance this is to have Mindfulness, to be Mindful. Many Souls find it hard to empty their minds when first starting Meditation but in time you will get over this road block, but it has been said that to empty the Mind is to deny its reality, as its only when you encounter the Mind and take heed of all levels of its contents, its then that we can experience a full all rounded experience of Life in all its richness, glory and splendor.

Part 13

Locating & Finding Your Imagination

When doing this Meditation exercise start off by focusing on a wooden chest with many draws built in it, as you see the chest in your Minds eye by visualizing it, now let your imagination take over and to allow objects to appear in the draws of the wooden chest these objects represent your feelings and thoughts.

If you find it hard to visualize at first when starting Meditation, then sit in front of a chest of draws with your eyes open visualize the chest and the amount of draws then close your eyes and see it, visualize it in the eye of the Mind in three dimensional pictorial image form.

So the wooden chest with draws it's

represents your Mind and when you open the draws there are objects inside, these objects represents your thoughts and feelings, what do you see, visualize in the draws of the chest, are there objects that represent things in your Life,
your behaviours, your moods, your emotions, your personality. Their will be random things that come up and don't make sense many of these will be from the UnConscious Mind.

Visualize taking each item out of the draws in the chest, what type of feelings do they relate to, what ever feelings come up relating to an object except them, and Meditate on them and if not happy with them make a change, let go of these old feelings that are holding you back and no longer serving you, other feelings that you cherish positive memories hold on to, put the objects back in the draws concentrate on breath for a while then open your eyes. Repeat this process in Meditations till your focus of Mental energy, makes it easy to access and you

are able to visualize with ease.
In Meditation when using our imagination it enables us to clearly focus and to deeply delve into our inner most feelings and thoughts, when we have clear focus in Meditation we can observe indepth the effect it has on you when you observe pictorial images and vibrational sounds, we all have the Eternal gift of Instant manifestation when we run at our optimal potential with the highest frequency vibration embodied, so we all have the gift the ability to make appear to conjour up and hold images in the Minds eye, it comes with ease with continuum of practice, so with dedication and most important discipline which we all fall off that wall along the life long learning of Meditation, it's a part of the process so don't be hard on your self, be patient it becomes easier over time, much easier in every moment of the present. Remember the end goal you will achieve your own realization of your fullest potential that of metamorphising into your natural Divine true Nature, that of an Eternal

Interdimensional Light being of Ultra Violet Enegetic Consciousness, so an Immortal Goddess or Immortal God, for we are all One in the Oneness of all Creation, the Brahman, the Whole, Namaste.

Part 14

Observing Our Emotions

Many people by nature are highly emotional and are used to experiencing very high levels of emotions, and Meditation can and will bring out your emotions so you can analyze them get to understand them and decihper them, then you will be able to control then through breath practices. Other people must prepare to perceive their emotions if they are the type of person to keep their emotions hidden away who keep them in check, if you are a person who is the unemotional type and are quite cool then this is an eventuality that you will have to face so just breathe through the process of watching and understanding your emotions in Meditation.

Through Meditation we see the emotions and are able to observe them and learn to understand them and that of their nature, and we can discover why they keep reoccurring and start to perceive their patterns and cycles, we can then control them when they come up and not allow them to Govern us or over whelm us. This will lead to a deeper understanding with focus with Meditation practice when we encounter and analize them then we can respond to them accordingly, in a more rational way with a calm approach. There are no psychological benefits in trying to gain control of your emotions or trying to fight them and even supress them, as its just pointless, its futile. When you start to feel and experience strong emotions in Meditation you will learn to develop a close relationship with them and see them for what they are, this will allow you to have a deeper relationship with your Inner Self, because as we monitor our emotions and perceive whether they are negative or positive, we become the observer in our daily lifes and also in Meditation, we see the triggers and the patterns and learn how to respond to them or in many cases the negative

emotions we don't respond to as we see this as old programming from our childhood and life experiences with others.
A therapeutic way of dealing with strong emotions that come up, is to write them down and with concentration we can express them in a positive way in a constructive way, as emotions held deep inside from past cycles and life experience can be over whelming at times as you learn to perceive and control them. If at times your emotions are taking over you allow them to fade away to die down and take a step back from your emotions, you can close your eyes and imagine you are being soothed by a bubble of Source light in its most powerful colour and vibration, that of Ultra Violet light and allow them to fade away, this is a good way to deal with extremly powerful emotions, then gradually they will be washed away and you will feel the inner turmoil dissipate, they will be driven away and cease to exist, then allow silence and an Inner Peace will encompass you.

Part 15

Dispelling Negative Emotions

In Meditation and in daily life this practice will allow you to control and deal with rising strong negative emotions, breathe deeply close your eyes breath calmness into your being and use a crystal as a representation of your troubled worries, hold the crystal that's attracted to you to dispel the negative emotions see in your Minds eye them leaving the Body and Mind and entering the crystal, and the crystal with absorb these unwanted negative emotions.

Allow the crystal to soak up all the negative feelings and thoughts from the Body and Mind when you are triggered by negative emotional responses and thoughts then they will die down, fade away and cease to exist any longer in that moment in the present then they can no longer trouble you. Then see with your imagination in your Minds eye that the crystal empties the negative emotions of thoughts and feelings, once you have come back to breath at the end of the Meditation and opened your eyes, go outside and put the crystal under the moon light for a couple of hours to cleanse the crystal then leave the crystal in the earth for several hours to let it recharge.

Part 16

Body Awareness & Mindfullness

Mindfulness involves becoming more aware of our Inner Selfs and that of our body, mind, feelings and thoughts, many people don't pay full attention of the body unless it is experiencing physical pain, they are disconnected its only discomfort that makes them aware of the body, we are not aware of its existance we walk the path of life detached from it, with Mindfulness we become attached to the body once more and can perceive the feelings and thoughts with a higher Awareness.

Meditation encourages us to have an inner relationship with our feelings and thoughts via our emotions, so we become aware of the different sensations we experience in daily life, we see them and then can be Mindful of them as we see them come up, we then clearly start to perceive the relationship to body and mind via the emotions and how they manifest and affect us physically and mentally. So we must learn to nurture them for our over all Physical, Mental and Spiritual well being, it is fundamental that we do so to have full health and balance creating an equilibrium in our entire being.

Part 17

Meditation While Walking

Meditating while walking does and will give you a rise in awareness and increase your relationship between your body and mind, this should be done in nature as when away from microwave signals your Luminous Energy Field will expand, be present in the moment being aware of the surroundings around you take it all in, and feel the ground beneath your feet, the air in your lungs be Mindful.

Walk freely where you don't have to avoid obstacles, and where there is not many people even alone is best to start walking Meditation.
When you are walking and present in the moment be deliberate and slow at a steady pace, be observeant and watch and feel your body and its movements while

in the process of walking, be focused be aware starting at your feet and move up your body, during this Meditation process ensure you are fully aware of how it feels to be inside of the Avatar the Human biological body. As thoughts come in allow them to just watch them see the cloud thoughts float on by, but focus on the walking be in a Meditive State, you will feel a calming and when your ready come back to your Awareness in this physical reality and finish your Meditation.

Part 18

Symbols & Their Power

The imagination is a powerful Creative Force and is called upon and is constantly being used in the Minds focal points when we use images, sounds and objects, this allows stimuli in the process of developing the Minds eye, this encourages improvement of your perceptions and your natural born Divine Chi Powers. This allows our perceptions to see beyond the boundries of the Conscious Mind, we start to see the Cosmic and Universal messages in the symbols, sounds, objects and images they mean something much deeper once you have contemplated them and dichipered them, there is a hidden language that lies deeper with in, there is knowledge and wisdom and truth of our true Universal reality and that of the multidimensional realities, the deeper coded messages become more they become reflections of a metaphorical.

These symbols in nature are highly useful tools in Meditations, ancient traditional symbols know as mandalas are used in focus of Meditation, mandalas further our journey in Meditation with good results with much progress. There is great power in the symbols they give the ability of giving a summary of several ideas at once at the same moment, some will be at times contradictory so this allows us to respond to symbols on multipule levels, and we can see a symbol change it grow it and our relationship will then adjust and change to that particular symbol. So the nature of symbols is all encompassing so that is why they are such powerful tools to use in Meditation, try it get a mandala pattern and practice experiment. A decorative and symmetrical diagram that is complex in its make up and was designed in the traditional practices of Hinduism and Buddhism, used in

Meditation to aid the practice, the mandala also represents the form of divine beings and that of the Cosmic Forces.

When Meditating there is no need to be specific in your interpretations of the mandala or of its meanings, you may perceive and feel a sense of stillness, peace and harmony beoming very tranquil, as sense of a connection to the Creation to the Oneness of the Cosmos in it entirety.

When Meditating on a mandala in Mindfulness in a high State of Awareness in th present completely mentally alert, no need to judge them in any way, when practicing with the mandala see them as gate ways in images and enter them walk through to the other side taking in the sights, sounds and features, and theres no need to worry or concern yourself with the Spiritual aspect their Spiritual significance, in these moments be a sponge and just absorb all you perceive in those moments, be fully present with alert Awareness.

Part 19

Vibrational Sounds & Picturial Images

We are able to explore our inner being through positive use of our senses of hearing and sight in all styles of Mediation practices, Meditation is creating a close relationship between the UnConscious and Conscious Minds and then we perceive beyond the reality we perceive in this moment in the present. Opening our selfs up to all possibilities and seeing our Minds the UnConscious and Conscious connected as One, with the stimulation of different images, objects and sounds, we can form this connection between the two Minds with our Chi Energy of imagination, we have the potential to change and evolve to raise our bodies vibration.

We expand our Minds and Consciousness

and we can influence it in positive ways with the extremely and tremendous creative power contained with in images and sounds when used and accessed in Meditation by the connecting of the two Minds the UnConscious and the Conscious mind.

Just like mantras which I love that we vocalize with phrases and words and when chanted in the right vibrational sound they are powerful and heal you benefit your well being raising your vibration. It took thousands of years for mandalas to be manifested and to evolve, many particular sounds and images are well know Worldwide, the geometry the geometric structure of mandalas are representations of the Cosmos, the Creation, the Brahman, the Whole.

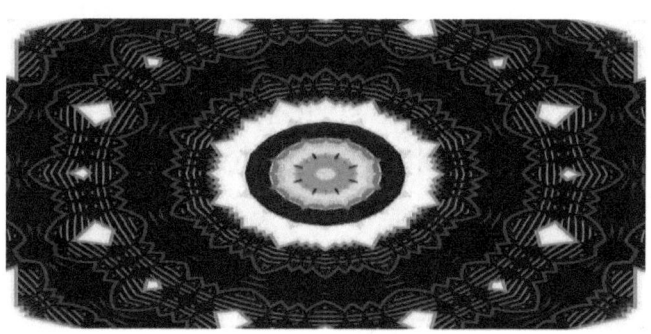

Part 20

Lotus Flower Meditation

To encourage your imagination to grow and expand a symbol of achievement and growth, when centered in stillness with the breath while Meditating see, visualize in your Minds eye the lotus flower, then imagine her growth from seed then growing to a seedling to a tall plant, and buds form with the nourishment of the rain water and the suns rays photosithsis energy, see in the Minds eye the potential of the bud as it will bloom and come fourth in to her true nature of beauty.

Visualize her blooming like in a time lapse video image style in the Minds eye, as the bud reaches her fullest potential, let the colours come to life with fragrent perfumes, she strengths but recognize her very delicate nature as well. Meditate on your own life blooming like that of the lotus flower, visualize and see you can full fill your own fullest potential, that of an embodied human being transending all time and space in the Universe and in the Whole of Creation, with a manifested Eternal Interdimensional Rainbow Light Body, then we are able to return home with out having to shed the body, known as death (but we know we can't die, we are Eternal Energy that just Metamorphises into another form) because the Human Mind built this construct to have and understand meaning of Life, but meaning is in the Mind, built in a framework, a construct to perceive the meaning of Existance the meaning of Life.

See the lotus flower as a part of you and representing your Inner Self that has been dying to come burst fourth into being, a being of strength, able to stand in your Divine power, enlightened empathetic, compassionate and loving, see yourself as an Angelic Light being at peace with all

Creation, with no enemies in this World or any other. A being manifesting beauty with Creations of magical wonder, with your Ultra Violet Light Energetic Consciousness.

Part 21

Meditation & Vibrational Sound

Our sense of sight in which we use is our main essential function of the senses, you could say fundamental infact, but the fact also is that our sense of hearing is as fundamental as well, and is very important in the Meditation States, there are many different vibrational sounds up and down the scale, many are effective in the training of focus on the Attention, and will put you into a deeper State of Meditation.

I found when I first started Meditation it was hard to focus my Attention when there was sounds, noises in my surroundings, it was a distraction at times frustrating and intrusive, but turn these distractions into a positive, its all Mind over matter, so allow those surrounding sounds to take you much deeper into the Medative State, in the future you will be able to sit in Meditation on the corner of a busy street and you will block out all sound distractions.

THE MULTIDIMENSIONAL SOUNDS OF NATURE

Nature also allows up to attain deeper States of Meditation by simply being sat in her, the vibrational sounds of the water running down stream and that as it falls over the water fall, the sound of the winds and gentle breezes, the sound of the ocean crashing on the beach shore or against the rocks and the sound of the trees swaying and their leaves rustling, this is because we are the same make up we are One in the Oneness of all we are fundamentally connected with Nature by design. Many people prefer to Meditate in Nature with the songs sung into being by the melodies of the variety of birds species, this brings them quick connection into deep Meditation, via the connection to Nature and that of our Mother Earth Pachamama.

Alternatively you can purchase a cd or down load music that represents natures sounds like the ones mentioned above even the ocean mammals, the whales and dolphins vibralional communication sounds are sublime, many people I know have used these to achieve a deeper Meditational State, see what works for you but I found very beneficial. This a good Nature connection Meditation to do before you start a walking Meditation.

Part 22

Visualised Healing

In this visualizing Meditation can be used in any moment to bring you back to the present, especially if you are out of tune, at odds with Self and are disconnected from the Mind, Body but especially Spirit. You can create your own Unifying Visualization by using the symbolic Principles of the mandala, then we can channel in and produce Zero Point Energy abilities.

Sit down in lotus position spine straight in the moment with the breath, close your eyes then relax your whole being, then visualize in your Minds eye a Universal symbol of Wholeness and also of healing, see a cross with a circle around it, so the visualization you need to see in the Minds eye, the symbol is divided into four quarters, perceive each quarter then visualize an image in each of them, then create and paint a picture in each quarter of the Cosmic symbol. While you are Meditating on this see Ultra Violet healing light coming from the centre of the symbol, and it shines upon you radiating you in Ultra Violet Cosmic healing light, illuminating your entire being to the Inner Core. Meditate on the Ultra Violet healing light as it pulses as it expands and intensifies, this fills you with a calming soothing your being inwards and outwards, see yourself in the present healed in full health. I use this even in the car an moment you feel your emotions rise go back to your breath, then light healing and an Inner Peace you will find.

I like to after opening Sacred Space and or being in my seventy two degree pyramid, I start to visualize golden white light Source Energy pouring into my Crown Chakra and filling the Whole of my Luminous Energy Field, then I connect to Mother Earths Chakra all the way down, then back from her centre through the larva, the crust plates then up through the bed rock, then up through the earth and into my Base Chakra with her energy filling my entire being, then I visualize connecting my Third Eye Chakra to my Heart Chakra with golden white light, then I can produce Ultra Violet light from my Heart Chakra, I then can fill my Luminous Energy Field that is a foot above the head, and a foot below the feet and as far as the arms can stretch outwards, this is powerful,l as we are in energy form Ultra Violet Light beings, our Consciousness is Ultra Violet Light, you can heal Self but even better you can visualize a friend or family member and see them in the Minds eyes, even in a particular location and with your attention send them healing in light form, say with every exhalation of breath I send Ultra Violet healing light to that named person and with every heart beat a pulse of Ultra Violet Light ripples out to heal them.

On the wWole of Creation perspective I

like to open and expand my Luminous Energy Field out past the Planet, the Solar System, the Galaxy, the Universe, Multiverses and I encompass all Multidimensional densities in Creation, including the highest realms outside time and space, the Immortal, Eternal realm where the Kingdom of Light resides, then after encompassing the Whole Brahman, I send the healing of Ultra Violet Light as I just mentioned from breath, the Heart Chakra and I do a flickering of the eyes, its an Ancient technique filling the Creation with Ultra Violet healing light. I then wish all beings great and small to find Inner peace, to project Outer peace, to have enlightenment, to create balance an equilibrium in the Creation, the Brahman, the Whole. Always pull your Luminous Energy Field back to around your Avatar your Human biological body before finishing the Meditation, its very powerful the light healing, using Conscious Chi Energy. Practice its exciting waking up to the possibilities of your fullest potential, I wish you all success on this Ascension journey home outside time and space in the Eternal realm, but at the same time being fully embodied on a fifth dimensional Planet, blessings Namaste I love it, it's awesome in it's Nature, Spirit Consciousness creating on a continuum.

Part 23

Practicing Continuum Affirminations

Affirmations in Meditation is a way to combat the negative infulences in our daily lifes and to counteract negative UnConscious thoughts that can be intrusive and have a negative impact in our lifes. Slowing down our Creative abilities to achieve our goals if not controlled the UnConscious Mind underminds our focus on Attention, so just come back to the breath and the calming will occur and Clarity you will see.

So you are trying with affermations to reprogram the UnConscious Mind, so you can be focused and present in every moment in the present now, make them specific to the point be direct with Self, they can be to bring in what to your life what you need to aheieve your goals, for me its all about accessing the Light Body, achieving Ascension, connection to Nature and Spirit, to travel the Hyper-Dimensional Light Time Matrix and Shamanic practices, and light work, as its what we are, its magical in Nature. Let your affirmations become your daily mantras through out your daily life, change will soon come be patient as you tap into your Eternal Chi Energy powers and gifts.

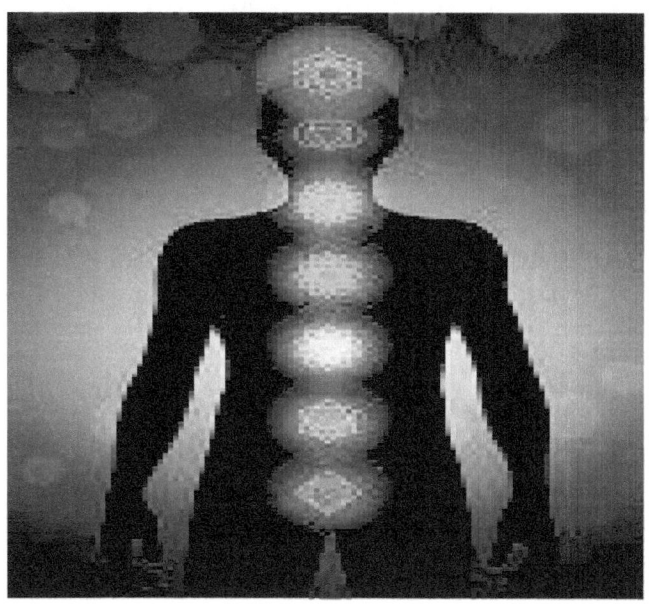

Part 24

Accessing & Tuning Into Vibrational Sounds

Vibrational sounds in the form of music are structural in a form of meaningful rythum and harmonies they are expressing and inexpressible forms of meaning, and penetrate the depths of the Human Soul and our depths and layers of our natures in expression of vibrational sound.

We can create positive associations in the right mood frame which allows us to focus the Mind, our brains respond happily to the musical language of vibrational sound and this is often amplified in nature with our Mother Earth Pachama's natural elemental sounds and of the creature sounds in Nature.

The UnConscious mind is influenced by certain ranges and scales of musical vibatory sounds which will raise Consciousness and uplift you even well known is if you listen to Mozart some of his selected extracts simulate Creativity and will relax you, chill you right out, I used to play Mozart in my poly tunnels of organic foods vegtables, herbs, fruits, medicine plants and I found their was an actual extra one quarter to a third extra growth leading to more fruits from the food plants, an amazing experiment with awesome results.

So find your space and experiment with Mozart and many other musical types and genres of vibrational sounds, while Meditating find what works for you personally, I love tribal music and especially Shamanic sounds of chanting and natural instruments, and also Buddhist mantras, these can have a profound affect upon you and lift you Spiritually, giving you an enlightening experience, but remember there is a difference to be distinguished between just relaxing to the music you listen to and actually Meditating to it, to deepen the Meditation State while in practice.

You can practice yourself playing different instruments singing different songs chanting, also wailing they are great ways to expess Ones Self, you can make your own recordings I do this myself when conducting Ancient Shamanic ceremonies and also out of ceremonies. I find my own recordings of my chanting, wailing, singing, drumming and other tribal instruments and affermations I put in some on repetative cycles bring me to a deeper Meditation, and bring a manifested life of there own that creates a mystical atmosphere, even a tribal connection to my Anscestors and to Spirit, a connection to the Eternal to the Sacred.

This will increase your concentration powers and improves your memory capabilities, and allow you to believe in your goals and attainments with confidence, it will help you to turn your attention on the present single aspect you are involved in in the moment allowing you to be more focused on a single attention, the focus of musical vibrational sounds leads to successful deeper Meditations.

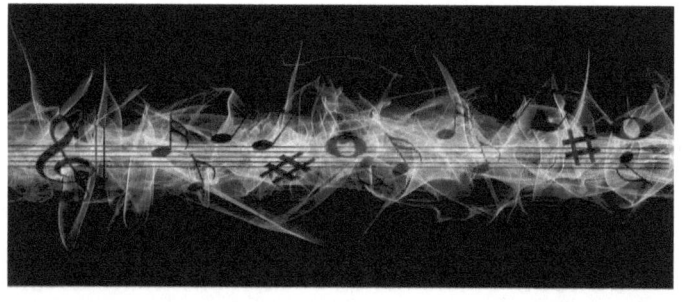

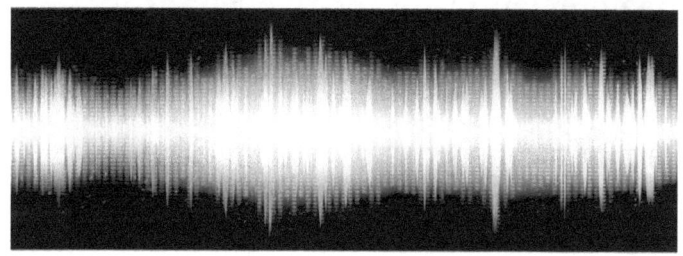

Part 25

Reflections Of The Moment

Meditations allow us to reflect and show us the importance of becoming the observer of self and that of our UnConscious Mind, the body and then the images and sounds we perceive in the Minds eye, this allows us to build the connection from the UnConscious Mind to the conscious Mind allowing us to decipher Ourself, and then access and process the Cosmic information we receive in Meditations, via images and sounds and in daily life, as subtle influences come in to manifestation after the connections of the two Minds is made.

Part of the process of Meditation is we perceive an apparent separation of the UnConscious and Conscious Mind this is true, we perceive to be seperated from the observer that observes the oberserved, but this is crutial in Meditation practice, initially as we focus attention on our physical, mental and Spiritual experiences, we later then combine them as One, then you realize ultimately the observer and the observed are One and cannot exist with out each other.

Remember when we are in breath we find stillness then Clarity, so when the Mind is calm and still, we become Mindful with a connection to Spirit to the Eternal and we get a sense of Wholeness and Unity, in the Oneness of all there be in Creation, this is the end goal to have a permanent connecting to the Oneness of all existence, connected to the Zero Point Energy Field of the Hyper-Dimensional Light Time Matrix accessing all of Creation. Meditation is one of the keys to gain access, also diet, mantra, prayer and ancient energy arts and practices like Shamanic ceremonies.

Meditation practices can take time for some people to access, I remember the Dalia Lama saying it can take one person thirty years of practice to achieve access, but another person may take thirty minutes it depends on the person. Meditation is the pursuit of a State of Oneness Consciousness it should come naturally and be effortless, some times the goal you wish to acheieve can be achieved by taking your Minds eye an aim off of a particular goal or achievement you wish to attain, this is talt in the Zen Meditation practices. After a while Meditating you will see the Medative State purely is for its own sake not for any particular end result.

When Meditating in a relaxed State with an open Mind and Heart space you will see antinomy, that is a logically Self contradictory statement or a statement that runs contrary to Ones expectation, it is a paradox, a statement that despite apparently valid reasoning from true premises, leads to a seemingly Self contradictory or a logically unacceptable conclusion, but this will allow you to achieve your desired goal in the present moment of now. You will then get from Meditation the positive results of mental, physical and Spiritual benefits, were you will reap your rewards for your dedication and discipline.

Meditation is also about patience in the attainment of awareness and becoming present in every moment in our daily life, to breath Meditation in every breath is to live a present life in the moment of now, for the present now is the only truth of existance, expressing its Self Individually and Collectively in the present moment of now, in all dimensions of Creation, all connected as One, One being of Oneness consciousness. Meditation should become your daily vibrational frequency and become your natural State of being and your natural beat and rythum of your Life Force.

Part 26

Beyond The Self

Meditation brings us into Awareness of all potentials and possibilities that we can manifest into our lifes, we perceive the Creation and our World not as just dualistic or polarized, we then learn and see it is both not either or but connected as One in Unity for it is the truth of the Oneness of Creation, we see we are Divine and we possess material and Spiritual dimension in the Self, coming from our Outer and Inner Worlds of our Consciousness from the Body and Mind, fuelled by Spirit that is the Eternal flame of all Creation. We step beyond the Maya of bounderies created by the Mind for meaning and understanding, and the oppositions dissolve away, and we perceive Meditation actually allows us to have growth in our lifes, especially Spiritual growth, this will make life easier as it becomes meaningful and Unifed, and then you will see the Sacred in all that surrounds you and envelopes you in existence in the Whole Cosmos, in the entire Creation.

We also through Meditation learn there is a paradoxical anecdote or even a riddle with out a solution, we see this demonstrates the inadequacy of logical reasoning to premote and prevoke an awakening in enlightenment. So one must break away from old cycles and patterns when contemplating, analizing and thinking about the apprehending World and that of Creation, the Brahman, the Whole.

When we contemplate the significance of the riddle or paradoxical anecdote, we see it's a conundrum and the solution is the response of intellectual impasses, that arise while engaging our Minds while in Meditation, Meditation is a tool to access information through sounds and images and allowing access to other dimension of realities and Consciousness, to attain the answers to solving the puzzle of Life, and that of manifested and non physical manifested matter of Creation.

The aim of Meditation is to point us in the direction of Wholeness and Oneness to guide us to Unity in Self and Collectively, we have to break the old patterns of thought and realize the continuum of conundrums indicate an under lying unity of opposites and see it as all United Connected and intertwined as One.

When Meditating the veil is lifted to reveal a profound mystical truth of reality in all dimensions of existence, once the many levels and layers of the two Minds of the UnConscious and Conscious Mind have been revealed and connected, the perception of our Inner Selfs and that of the Creation lead us to enlightenment, and then on to evolving and metamorphosis into that of an Angelic Light beings, and so we take the path to

Ascension then onto Transcending in the Hyper-Dimensional Light Time Matrix of Creation.

Remember you must look within, with much contemplation with stillness, but you must stay grounded and humble also, and you will manifest and achieve all of your wishes bringing to life physical matter, Creations of beauty, magic and wonder for all to see in the Creation, the Brahman, the Whole.

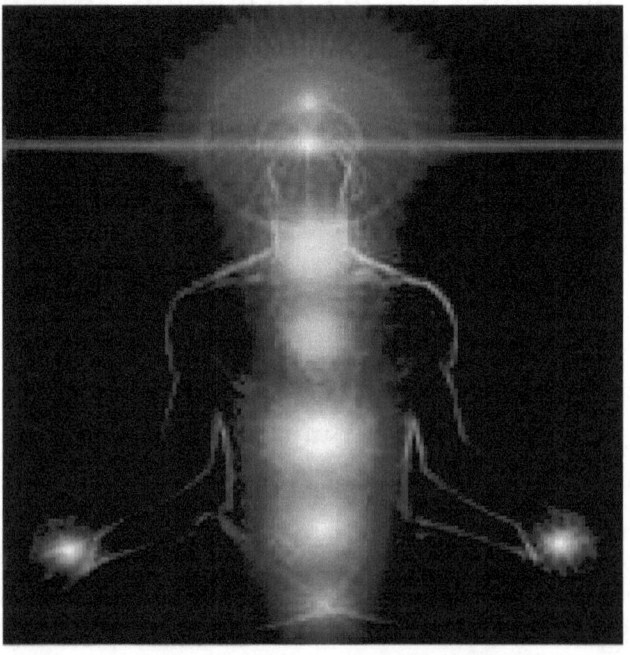

Part 27

Who Is The Eternal I

It is important to find our Inner Self to reveal our true identity and that of our true Eternal Nature, it can be challenging in the body of emotions with a Monkey Mind and in a World of chaos, deceit, lies, manipulation and with illusionary distractions of bright flashing lights and with a wide range of vibatory soothing and interactive sounds, all designed to distract you from the true nature of reality, here on Planet Earth, and from the other Star Nations, from other dimensions that exist in and out of your informational DNA gene pool, for within your DNA is the Schematics, the Blueprint to grow your Eternal Light Body.

We start to ask the questions to our Inner Selfs like where have I come from, where am I going, who am I, where and how do I fit in the bigger scheme of things in the Creation, what is my purpose, we start to comprehend and focus our attention on the most sort questions of life, the actual important and fundamental questions of life and existence. So we have to open up possibilities that had not existed previously before but are available in the present, we learn there are no direct clear cut answers its not that simple, but over time and with a deep continuum of Meditation answers you seek will come with Clarity, then we fall away from being blind in ignorance and we then attract and gain understanding, insight and enlightenment through the Ancient Wisdom and Knowledge we access from the Hyper-Dimensional Light Matrix from the Cosmic Consciousness of the Whole from the Oneness of all that be.

Through Meditation your true identity will shine fourth and your Eternal Consciousness with come to the fore front of your being, this will over time in the now on a continuum gradually and will be known, for you will recognise the changes as they occur within, during your rise of Consciousness and your growth Spiritual as you connect to the true reality of Creation, in the Light Time Matrix and beyond in the Eternal realms.

We must learn to understand that we are the past, the present and the future all at the same time in the now, and as the Eternal Immortal Soul in a manifested Human Avatar biological body, that we are having a Human Intellectual, emotional, physical and Spiritual existence all connected as One, we have the four bodies the physical body, the mental body, the emotional body and the Spirit body, once all are joined, United, Unified, connected as One in sync, we can access our Light Bodies our optimal potential as Human beings, this is the climax at the end of the manifesting continuum cycle of reincarnation on a particular Planetry body, before the chance to graduate to a higher dimension,

this is called Ascension.
We learn our past experiences and memories from this life and one that came before create our Individual Psyches, this comes from the many things we have studied and retained in the past and things long forgotten, but also know that we have had a long process of evolution and belonged to many races, species, to all their narrative of histories and lived their ways in their Civilizations, ultimately all these experiences have formed our Individuality of our Psyches and we access this level of our Consciousness via the level of Spirit through our Eternal Spirit Consciousness, this is just a part of the comtinuum of evolution is is the process by way of manifesting into the physical realms of matter to grow Spiritually.

In Meditation we also have to bring our focused attention on the Collective Consciousness of Humanity, and also eventually focus on the Whole Consciousness of the Oneness

Consciousness, that encompasses all of the Creation, for alive every cell and partical be.

When in Meditation and tuned in to the Cosmic energies we perceive and can connect to the Zero Point Energy Field, we call Source Energy often referred to as Prana Energy, this is the circulating Life Force Energy that be inherent in all things, with a balance of negative and positive forms, all possibilities of all potentials come fourth and can be manifested instantaneously. We must learn to harness this Cosmic Chi Energy and we can draw upon support from Light beings and collect Ancient Wisdom and Knowledge, also gaining strength allowing us to stand in our Divine Power, this gives us an Inner knowing of our connection to all in the Cosmos, and an Eternal deeper sense of the Immortal Self, and that of the many character roles you played, by manifesting on a continuum in this Universe for the last thirteen point six eight billion years, this gives you a deep sense of belonging Internally and Externally when you wake up Consciously to the Oneness Consciousness.

Then We Can Connect To The Zero Point Energy Field & Transverse The Cosmos In Our Light Bodies.

Part 28

Burning The Past Away

To move forward in life to create change we must learn to grow and evolve to do this we must burn the past away, I do this for myself and others during Shamanic fire ceremonies, write down on two pieces of paper the things you need to remove from your life and on the other piece of paper write what you want to bring into your life, you start with the burning of the things to remove from your life you can read it out loud if you wish to give it more energy, as your cells are listening at the level of the tetrahedrons that bring fourth your manifestations, then place in fire with you focused Chi Attention on your Intention, then have a moment and contemplate these things removed from your life, then focus your attention on the positive things you are bringing into manifestation and put that into the fire and then have some moments in contemplation with your intention on the positive things you wish to bring into your life.

Letting go of the past in a Meditation State sit in lotus position spine upright focus on breath, once stillness is attained focus your attention on your awareness, visualize your earliest memories and experiences and the feeling the emotions that they stired within and if they don't serve you in the present release them let them go, delete them from your Luminous Energy Field, that is the Software that informs the Hardware the DNA to grow the physical body, go in to the deepest depths of your Inner Self in the smallest recesses of your UnConscious and Conscious Mind, and tell yourself I remove them, I release my past I am ready to move in to the new possibilities of all potentials, I delete the past from my Luminous Energy Field and so it be by the Eternal Divine Energy within me and I make it humble so now in the present moment, namaste.

You can Meditate on them individually and release them one by one with a focused Attention on your Intention, when you are in this Meditative State it is a sacred space a powerful space of manifesting these releases of the past cycles that no longer serve you in the present, when you done this and ready to leave Meditation, come back to breath find the stillness and as you calm and Inner Peace comes over you, you will smile with Clarity in Mind, open your eyes, take a moment then continue with having a blessed day.

Part 29

Accepting New Manifestations

This Meditation is about accepting new manifestations to come in to your life and except the changes that will occur, and allow you to focus your attention of bringing in the new and leaving the old burnt away in the past, for it no longer will serve you as you awaken to your fullest potential of accessing your Light Body by Metamorphosizing to your Divine Natural State of being but also fully embodied. So sit in stillness in lotus position or on a chair in unable to physically, spine straight in silence in the breath eyes closed, and what ever comes to you in this Meditation just except it for what it is, come to focus your Awareness on the changed State of your now opening up Mindfulness and perceive any changes and their connected feelings, just breath and it will come to you naturally in an organic fashion. Focus your Awareness to not have any judgements on the thoughts and feeling you experience as they come fouth into your focused attention, let your response be an openness to accepting new manifestations in your life, openly accept the changes coming in to your manifest surrounding and Internal manifest changes that are occurring within and without your being. Be in the moment develop that non judgemental point of view or approach to analizing your thoughts and feelings and also with visionary images, symbols and vibrational sounds, just accept them for a moment perceive them and let them drift away in your Minds eye, let them float on by to the back of your Mind, or even delete them if not serving you anymore just visualize the thought and feelings and vanquish them like particles until dissolved, this has worked for me, on my Meditation path on the Ascension time line I have chosen to manifest into Creation.

Part 30

The Oneness Of All Interconnectedness

(The decipher code here is ly changed to lee finding the fun magic of playing with language of words, ha love it awesome mystical they can be to describe nature of being, of reality and the nature of existence.)

In this World on this Planet Gaia, our Mother Earth our Pachamama, the way Society has been set up structurally in all facets and levels of control over Society by a few, then creating a negative damaging low vibrational environment to live in, well this can lead to a feeling of isolation and a sense of separation, this can be on the Individual level, as our conditioning programming indoctrinationand brain washing from this Planetry Culture based on false scientific Principles and built on materialism, this Culture by nature pushes an agenda of necessary conditioning, with the polarity of observer and observed this we were talt as seeing and percieveing the Universe as objectively, but we know that there is more much more powerful way of perceiving and decphiering the Universe and Creation via your Consciousness, via your third eye and via your Chakra Systems connecting them to the Universal Chakras and then in turn to the Zero Point Energy Field.

In Meditation the fundamental and profound ways of the themes of Interconnectedness, Wholeness and Oneness are a standard experience in Medtitations for this is part of the true nature of the Cosmic reality, we are connected on all frequencies, light, vibrations, energetic energies, and on all Spiritual levels too, we are also connected on a Soul contract level as well from our higher dimensional Selfs, manifesting in agreements to help teach and care for each other, to be teachers and students of each other for we are One in the Oneness of all Cosmic magical Conscious Energy, dancing Individually, but truly we are Unifed as One web Interconnected woven in the fabric of time and space, a Conscious construct of Light fFelds fluxing, pulsing and ever expanding, always contracting and evolving in the magical nature of the Divine Energies of the cCsmic Creation, the Brahman, the Whole. In Meditation we find all of the above true and see in the Minds eye we can travel in the Hyper-Dimensional Light Time Matrix via our energetic Light Bodies when activated, via Ultra Violet Energetic Divine Consciousness.

So Body and Mind, the Internal and External, the UnConscious and Conscious are all One connected and symbiotic in their relationship and in their nature of Eternal Spirit, this has an effect on the way we recognize the meaning and how we grasp the understanding of the realities of the World, Universe, Cosmos, the Whole Hyper-Dimensional Matrix that surrounds and encompasses in the Oneness of all that be in the Whole of Creation, for we all have an Inner and Outer Interconnectedness to each other and to all densities and forms of energetic light, vibrating at multipule frequencies, its just a wonder, a magnificent Creation, as you ponder in contemplation, almost at its mystical qualities and you perceive that its a marvel, an illusionary phantasm that is the construct of a mental representation of the manifested physical structured construct of the matter realities, in all of Creation built via the Cosmic elemental forces of electromagnetism, the strong and weak nuclear forces and gravity, the Divine Conscious Energy of Spirit. We also see there are no remarkable coincidences when meeting, events and encounters manifest in the present moment in the now, and we realize every encounter is charged with energy of meaning, if we take notice and are present in the moment, we become aware and place our attention on the encounter we are having, there are subliminal subtle messages for you to decphier in Nature, in the Cosmos, in light energy forms, because nothing happens by chance it happens by observation with an Intention causing manifestation in One form or another.

Part 31

Meditation Of Kindness & Lovingness

In this Meditation you will practice outwardly what you practice internally it will give you the courage and strength and the ability to perceive that one must forgive ones Self for all mistakes for they were lessons to be learned for our growth in life and in evolution, we must start to truly love our self with understanding from compassion and empathy, the forgiveness at the level of intention of the Eternal Spirit.

Sit spine up right in lotus position or if unable sit on a chair, concentrate on bringing yourself into the present moment find stillness in the eye of your Mind, focus on the breath start with a few deep ones then have relaxed breath control,

Meditate on the Cosmos being Interconnected as One, and then pause and remember all the past moments you were unkind and others were unkind to you, recall the incident, the location the time frame in your Minds eye and let it go, as there is no need to hold on to it any longer as it does not serves you any more it just holds you back. Now Meditate on the Cosmos again being Interconnected as One and its continuum of constant connection to the Oneness in Creation, now say in your Minds eye you forgive the others that were unkind to you and you forgive yourself for being unkind to Self through the challenging and tough and ofton painful experiences we go through in this life time, tell yourself you end that cycle of negative manifestation and promise Self with your full Chi Energy Intention, to transform your manifestations into a positive outcome and not allow those types of feelings to manifest from your emotional body and you will not allow the UnConscious Monkey Mind to take you of your path of enlightenment and Ascension. That you will be kind loving compassionate and have understanding for others and self, and to be present in the moment in the now, to have a constant state of Mindfulness in all moments of now, in the Eternal ever lasting continuum of manifesting Divine Energetic Chi Cosmic Consciousness in the Whole of Creation. Then clear your Minds eye find silence, then peace will come and with breath for a while focus your Awareness in the present and open your eyes, you should feel rejuvenated and relaxed and very tranquil.

Part 32

Our Spinning Core Energy Chakras

Many cultures and ancient traditions perceive and view the body in a natural holistic multidimensional way, understanding that there is a fundamental force of energy that is recognized as essential to the Inner Energy Systems the Chakras, they are along the spine ancient texts explain them as spinning wheels of energy, the Chakra System that controls the flow and outward projection of your Chi Energy, they are in some Shamanic and tribal tradition seen as archetypes, so perceived as mental images these are also present in the Collective UnConscious, and related to a Spirit animal. The different Chakras also represent Inner qualities we attribute to our characters like compassion, strength, being loving, empathy for others and ourselfs and humility, working on these qualities and relationg them to the Chakras in the Minds eye during Meditation, just Unifies your Body, Spirit, Mind and Consciousness as One multifunctional, multidimensional being, working at optimal levels with focused attention therefore manifesting from a place of Clarity, with positive Intention.

Each Chakra is related to a particular part or several parts of the body, they are also related to a colour which is a certain vibrational frequency of light vibrating at a certain density, creating light in colour structural energy form. We must explore the Chakras and learn to channel the energy flows at the right rate of speed, so put your attention on their associations, move and direct energy flow towards the Chakra Centres, through the Medridian Energy flow Systems and explore their capabilities with practice and with dedicated Meditations on a continuum, you will attain your desired out comes, with the right Intention when manifesting in this structured Creation.

Sit down in lotus position spine straight or in a chair if uncomfortable in lotus position, come to breath take few deep ones close your eyes silence the Mind then focus your attention on your Chakras, get to know them their associations and subtle energy flows, visuilize them spinning with their torus field centres, see in your Minds eye your chakras spinning at a faster rate of speed as you unblock any negative blockages in the Meridaian energy flow System, to allow a continuous flow of unitrupted energy, keeping your Avatar Human biological body vibrating at a high frequency level, and raising your Consciousness, connecting you to the Creation via the Zero Point Energy Field. But when doing this focus on starting at the base of the spine with the Root Chakra and rising up the Chakras one by one, then work your way up through the Sacral Chakra just below your belly button, then move up to your Solar Plexes Chakra at the middle of the stomach level, then onto the Throat Chakra, then oto the Third Eye Chakra, and finish at the Crown Chakra which is located outside the body floating just above your head, then breath, then focus attention and your awareness back in your Meditation space, a few more breaths and open your eyes.

This Meditation will gain you access to your Core Chi Power manifesting at a rapid pace, with higher levels of Consciousness gaining Wisdom and Knowledge of enlightenment, and giving you access to the Hyper-Dimensional Templar Light Time Matrix, so you can Ascend and then Transcend at will instantaneously travel in your Light Body's sixty foot field of light, travelling through the sun filaments or by instant teleportation, remember you are a Divine angelic Light being Eternal on a continuum of being.

Part 33

Your True Nature

I started to look into Buddhism at fifteen years old but really dived in and studied it at seventeen so much ancient wisdom and knowledge I was sucked in, then I studied some of the Vedic texts from India, the Sanskrit word Buddha means awakening or coming to, as in waking uo and raising your Consciousness, finding enlightenment, then as time pasted its meaning was known as Spiritual awakening, this is when we ascertain our true nature that of a Buddha nature.

Buddha wrote a doctrine called the four noble truths in which he forms the basis of Buddhism, he examines the human condition and also prescribes the cure, the path we must take to acheieve Nirvana the transcendent State of Consciousness in which there is neither suffering, nor sense of self, desire, and the subject or being is released from the effects of Karma and released from the cycle of death and rebirth, it is the final attainment to achieve in the goal of Buddhist practice.

The life story of Buddha reveals that it was through the forms of the four truths that he attained enlightenment, through our understanding of our selfs as individuals in our true nature can we arrive at the awareness of the Universal truths of manifested life and that of the Whole Creation, the four truths explain all mortal life involves suffering, sickness aging and dying, the second truth says suffering is caused by our desires, the third truth is that when we eliminate desire, we stop all of our suffering, and the fourth truth offers a means to release all suffering. Then there is the eight fold path, which identifies eight factors that will lead you away from suffering and bring you into enlightenment, these factors the elements of concentration, wisdom, moral conduct as the main teachings in Buddhist lessons.

Our beliefs, our morals, our attitudes to death and our attitudes to life, our aspirations are all a craving from the individual creating a rise in suffering, in Buddhism they say we can not see the Universal truths because we are asleep in a Dream World. So we do not accept the truth even when its present in our surroundings, we are all apart of the Whole of Creation we are not separate or individual or self contained, we are connected and will return from where we came when we pass over, if you don't access your Light Body in this life time and access the Ascension path, then back around you go on another twenty six thousand yrear cycle of Karmic Incarnation.

Through Meditation, we can find our true nature through focus of Awareness and we perceive the realization that life is just as it is, in this Conscious Awakening everything remains the same, nothing changes only your attitudes to life evolves and is channelled in on the manner in which we conduct our selfs on this lifes journey.

CHAPTER FOUR

Accessing The Light Body The MUNAY-KI Nine Rites Of Initiation

Munay-Ki comes from a Quecha word that means (I love you, be as you are), these are the nine rites of initiation taken to become a person of wisdom and power, who will and has excepted the stewardship for all Creation. These rites are standard or common in all Shamanic traditions, though they are expressed in different ways, practices, forms and styles in different cultures. They originally come from the great initiations from the Hindus valley that were brought to the American lands by the first medicine men and women, who crossed the baring straights from

Siberia during the glacial period 30,000 years ago, these Old Earth Keepers were the known as the Laika, Earth Keepers of Old.

The Laika have always been ordinary men and women who have lived extraordinary lives, not born with special gifts from Spirit, but have acquired grace, power through prayer, study of ancient wisdom teachings and through discipline.
Some evolved to become leaders and healers while others lived quiet lives, growing crops and raising a family. The Laika felt, so knew people would come to the Munay-Ki when they felt a calling to do so, as I did myself.

Many of us have had that calling from Spirit and long to make a difference to your life and there for a difference in the world, as your manifestations create a part of this reality this World.

When you start on the path of the Earth

Keepers with sincere intention and with an open heart, you notice there are many around you, like you and your not alone. You find yourself in the company of other Earth Keepers that manifested on Earth many thousands of years ago, they are Luminous beings of light who are now woven in the fabric of time in the Hyper-Dimensional Matrix of life. These Earth Keepers of old will assist you in transformation with guidance, and combine there power and vision with your power and vision.

As you learn and start to practice the Munay-Ki you will feel the presence and sense the wisdom of these Luminous Ones who have stepped out of liner time and dwell in Sacred time, outside timelines and space, in Infinity, free from rebirth free from Karma.

The Munay-Ki nine rites clear your Luminous Energy Field of Psychic sludge left from life times of trauma.

It will raise your bodies vibration levels, these Luminous Ones are our guides.

These Earth Keepers come from the future, and can help us access who we are evolving to as humans, memories from the past and the visions of the future come as possibilities because everything in the future is in potential form.

That is why Earth Keepers from the tribes of the Inca, Hopi, Maya and there are many other Nations of old that gather in prayer to envision peace on Earth. They track different possible future timelines, to find the timeline with clean clean rivers and clean air with people living in harmony with nature and each other, a time line were we are reconnected to our true nature, peaceful, loving.

The visioning installs it into our Collective destiny and makes it more likely to manifest, when we connect and join the Earth Keepers from the future, we then have available to our selfs knowledge that will upgrade our DNA.

The Earth Keepers the Laika understand that our genes are not just informed by the past experiences and not just informed by our ancestors DNA, they understand that when you are free of the bounds of time and space, the future, your future self can reach backwards like a huge hand and pull you you forward in to who you are becoming, an awakened Luminous Light being, vibrating in love and light, moving through the veil of time and space and Infinity.

When you receive the nine Munay-Ki rites your Chakras will begin the brighten, to glow with their true original radiance and will develop into a Rainbow Light Body, in time with meditation and fire ceremonies to grow the seeds planted in your Chakras into fruit bering trees.

Then you can download a new better version of Software that informs your Luminous Energy Body, that will then inform the Hardware the DNA, with instructing on how to create a new body, that will heal, age and die differently, amazing I love it awesome, happy days.

All you have to do is invite these Luminous Ones, the Earth Keepers in when you are ready to to so, ready to receive them, they are our medicine lineage, they evolved from humans to that of Angels, some are Spirit, some are in bodies but they all have a mandate to protect those who are looking after and protecting and in balance with our Mother our Planet Earth, Gaia, Pachamama.

They are the greatest, finest Spiritual allies one can have, we can access the blue print in our DNA and grow and develop Luminous Energy Fields that of Angels in our life time, in the now, the Munay-Ki rites offers us access to energetic keys to allow us to do this, in the now.

As we become earth Keepers, we join the ranks of Angels from different Worlds and were the Original Souls present after Creation, they do not cycle through bodies as humans do, they have ever lasting life and are the Keepers of many Worlds, Galaxies and realms.

There were nine Munay-Ki rites that were given by ancient teachers of old given to them by Angelic beings and are now passed on from teacher to student, when the rites are passed on, it is a lineage of Luminous beings that transmits itself, that leaps from forehead to forehead. To transfer this energetic information, the Earth Keeper simply maintains Sacred Space and embodies the vibration of the level the or she wishes to transmit.

These initiations can not be done on your own, once you have received them, the rites are yours to transmit to others, there is One Sacred rule or there is one caveat, the rites are offered as a gift, free of charge, you may except gifts or donations or you may charge a fee for your time to coach someone as they go through the changes the Munay-Ki brings, but you can not charge for the rites themselves, they are Sacred for all in the Oneness to access, to evolve.

FOUNDATION RITES

Healer Rite – connects you to a lineage of Luminous beings from the past, who come to assist you in your personal transformation.

Awakens the healing power in your hands so that everyone you touch is blessed, there is tremendous Spiritual assistance available and these Luminous Ones work in our sleep to heal the wounds of the past and of our ancestors.

Bands Of Power & Protection – Five luminous belts are woven into your Luminous Energy Field for protection, they act as filters, breaking down any negative energies that come towards the person into one of the five elements, these energies then feed the Luminous Energy Field instead of harming.

Harmony Rites – Transmission of 7 archetypes into the Chakras , these are serpent, jaguar, hummingbird, and eagle and the 3 archangels -the Keeper of the lower World – the Keeper of the middle World and the Protector of the upper World, these 3 relate to our UnConscious, Conscious and higher Conscious Selves.

Seers Rite - Extra – cerebral path ways

of light are installed that connect the visual cortex with the third eye and heart Chakra, this awakens the inner seers in you and then have the ability to perceive the invisible World of energy and Spirit.

LINEAGE RITES

Day Keeper Rites – You will connect to a linage of Master healers from the past, the Day Keepers are able to call on the ancient altars to heal and bring balance to the World to Earth and bring humans into balance and harmony with nature and Mother Earth, they are the midwives, herbalists and Curanderos, this rite starts to heal the your inner feminine, to step beyond fear and practice peace.

Wisdom Keeper Rite – You will connect to a lineage of Luminous beings from the past and future, who hold wisdom of the ages from all societies and cultures, this rite allows you to heal your inner masculine, step outside liner time, become enveloped, steeped in the medicine and wisdom teachings and taste Infinity.

Earth Keeper Rite – This rite connects you to the Archangels they are the Guardians of our Galaxy, they are the Stewards of all Life on Earth, this rite connects you to the Sun, to our local Star and to the Stars beyond, it allows you to learn the ways of the Seer and then allows you to dream the World into being.

RITES OF THE TIME TO COME

Star Keeper Rite – This rite anchors you safely to the time afer the great change occurring, starting around 2012, you connect to your future Self and your physical body begins to evolve, the ageing process is slowed and your DNA is re-informed with light and you become more resistant to disease.

Creators Rite – Awakens the Creator light within and brings fourth a sense of Stewardship for all Creation, from the smallest grain of sand to the largest Cluster of Galaxies in the Universe, once attained only through direct transmission from Spirit, it is now possible to transmit from one person to another.

As you work with the germination of the seeds in your Chakras and put light the element of fire into them you will access your blueprint in your DNA and grow a Rainbow Light Body, Joining or returning to the Eternal realm, so you must do ceremonies and germinated the seeds of these rites and you will be touched by and be blessed by Angels, you only have to open yourself to the wisdom of the wise Luminous Ones, the Earth Keepers of Old and all will be bestowed upon you.

THE GREAT PRINCIPLES

Non – violence --- Bring no harm to yourself or others.

Truthfulness – Be true to your word and let your word be true, if you speak enough, what you say comes true.

Integrity – Do not steal, not even a glance, walk your talk.

Moderation – Use the life force within you wisely, don't waste energy.

Generosity – Give more than you take, for nothing in this world really belongs to you.

I hope this knowledge plants a seed with you and start your Munay-Ki journey blessings love life lee.

All I wish for is to see my fellow light being sisters and brothers to have enlightenment, to open there rainbow bodies of light, to stop the cycles of life and death, to ascend, to evolve to Homo-Luminus, to quantum leap ten thousand years into the future, into who you are becoming, who you are waking up to, the Immortal Inter-Dimensional Light being , for you are an Eternal Angelic being of Light, a being of Spirit for Eternal you be.

All I wish is for all humans and all species in this Universe to have Inner Peace, to project Outer Peace into the Creation, to bring healing and balance in the Brahman, the Whole, the Creation. Blessings on your Spiritual journey, blessings to all life in the Creation of Oneness, for Oneness is all there be, Namaste LoveLifeLee.

Learn how to Meditate gaining your Chi Eternal Inner Power accessing your Meridian Energy Systems, then accessing your Chakra Systems allowing you to access your Immortal Light Body and allowing you to access the Universe, the Creation, the Cosmos, the Kingdom of Light outside time and space, accessing the Whole Hyper-Dimensional Matrix, for the truth is, we are Eternal Inter-Dimensional Divine Rainbow Light beings of Ultra Violet Energetic Consciousness we are Angels, Goddesses and Gods. Please come join us on the path to enlightenment and ascension, transcend, quantum leap metamorphosing to your natural Eternal State of Being, Namaste LoveLifeLee.

There are many types of Meditation in this book and Meditation practices, Ancient Wisdom and Knowledge I have studied from Worldwide cultures and I have gained in my own Meditation practices and in my Shamanic practices and ceremonies, also I gained knowledge via Plant Medicines like Ayahuasca, Magic Mushrooms, Salvia Divinorum, DMT (Dimethyltryptamine), and from Astral traveling, out of body experiences and by entering the Eternal realms outside time and space, our true home we are trying to Ascend back to, the Divine realms of the Kingdom of Light.

There is focus on attention of the UnConscious Mind and Conscious Mind and their relationship, a concentration on breath work and accessing your Light Body via your DNA Blueprint, the Schematics to your Eternal Rainbow Light Body, accessed via Meditation, breath, diet, and your Consciousness, Namaste LoveLifeLee.

The next two images that follow are of the Human Light Body.

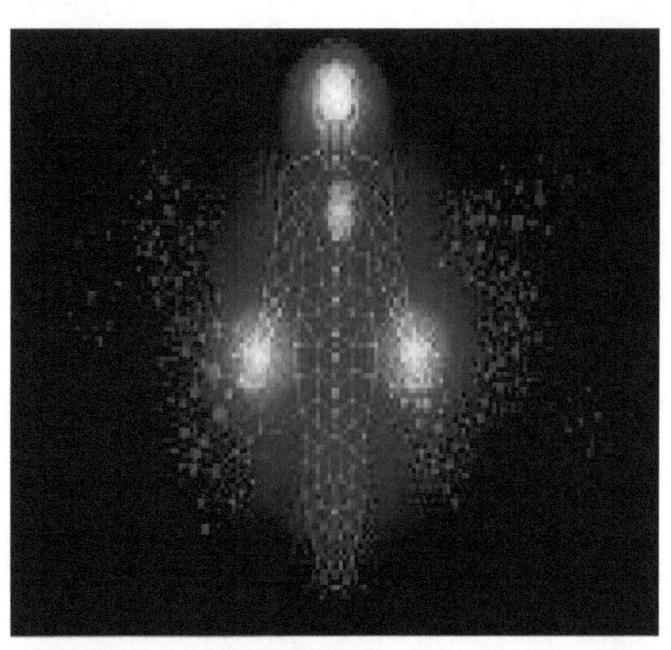
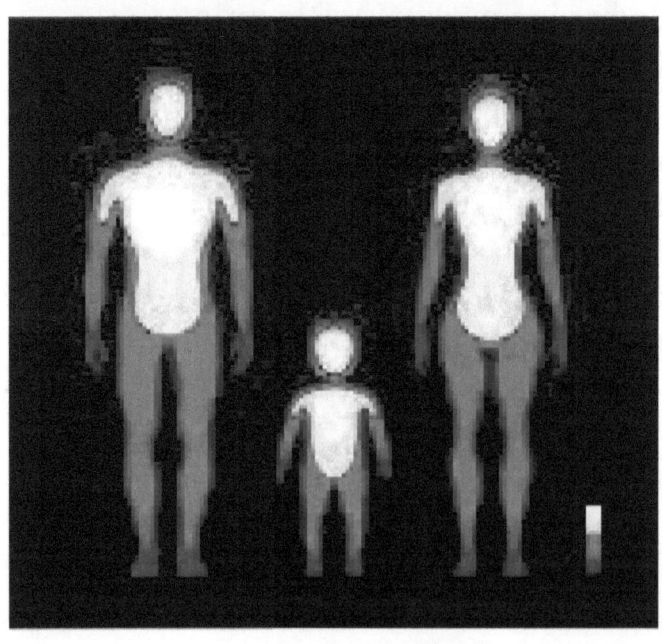

Other Books By Love Life Lee

Other Books By Love Life Lee

Other Books By Love Life Lee

Other Books By Love Life Lee

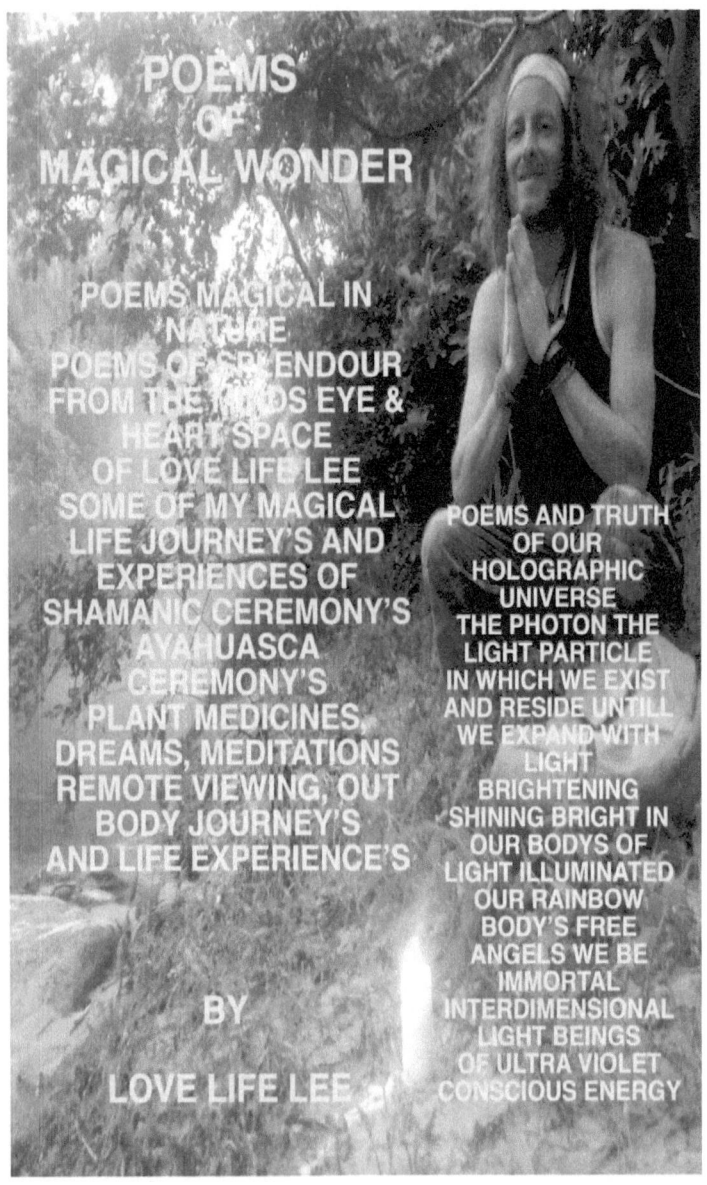

Other Books By Love Life Lee

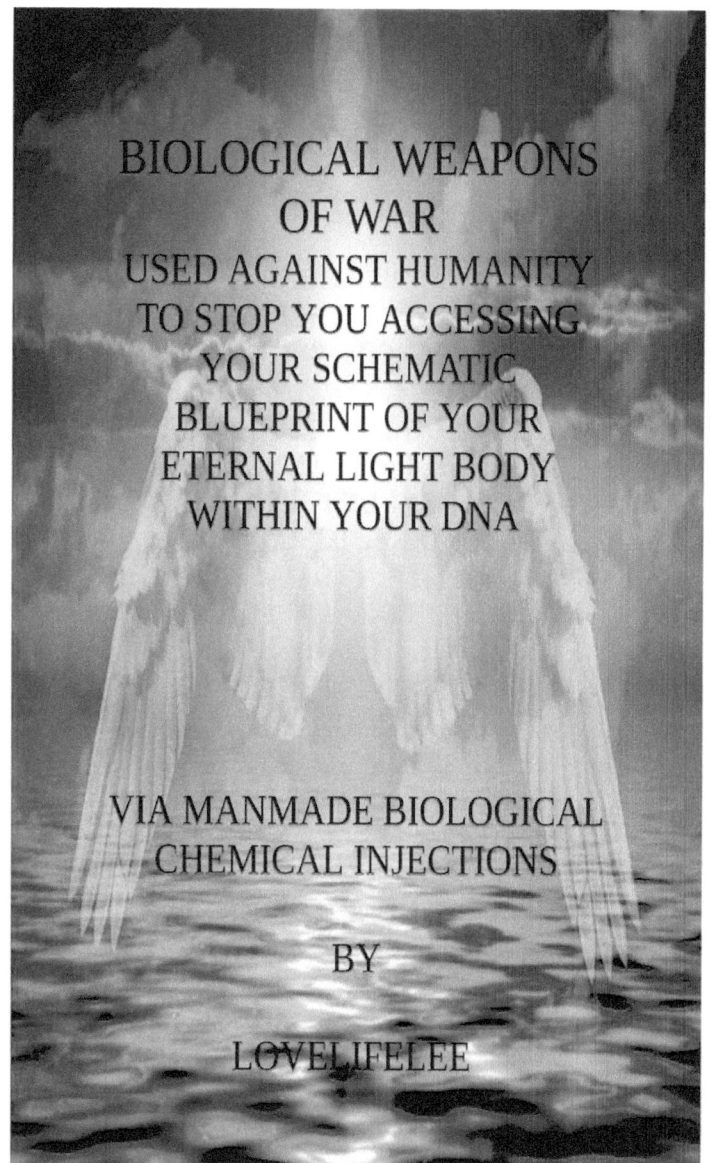

Other Books By Love Life Lee

THE TRUTH OF BIOLOGICAL CHEMICAL WEAPON INJECTIONS

& NASAL INOCULATIONS VIA TESTS & THE NEW NANO TECHNOLOGIES BEING INJECTED INTO HUMANITY TO PURPOSELY MAIM HARM KILL & REWRITE YOUR DNA ALTERING YOU TO TRANSHUMANISM WITHOUT YOUR CONSENT BY THE DISGRACED FALLEN ANGEL DESCENDANTS THEIR INTENTION TO HAVE A SMALL TRANSHUMANISM SLAVE POPULATION & THEIR MASS GENOCIDE ON HUMANITY & THE INGREDIENTS & THE PERPETRATORS & AUTOIMMUNE RESPONSES & FUTURE NEURMBURG TRIALS & AN INTRODUCTION TO GROW YOUR ETERNAL LIGHT BODY

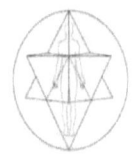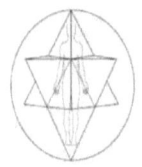

BY
LOVELIFELEE

Index Page

P 1-2 Book Title, Publishers Information FEEDAREAD.com Where Love Life Lee Books are Available.

P 3-8 Other books by LoveLifeLee.

P 9 The Eight Principles of Creation.

P 10-39 Chapter One The Hidden Knowledge, Manifesting a New Mindset & The Eight Fundamental Principles Of Creation.

P 40-55 Chapter Two The Great Work, An Introduction To The Human Eternal Light Body.

P 56-191 Chapter Three

Part –

1 An Introduction To Mediation.

2 – Realizing the connection between the body & the mind.

3 – Why meditate what is meditation.

4 – Meditation with a candle, Unwind relax loosen the body.

5 – Meditation and the breath.

6 – The development of your focus.

7 – Centre you self.

8 – Thought watching.

9 – Visualization in the eye of the mind.

10 – The way of life in meditation.
11 – Having an audience with your mind, becoming the listener & viewer.
12 – Becoming aware of mindfulness.
13 – Locating and finding your imagination.
14 – Observing your emotions.
15 – Dispelling negative emotions.
16 – Body awareness and mindfulness.
17 – Meditation while walking.
18 – Symbols and their power.
19 – Vibrational sounds and pictorial images.
20 – Lotus flower meditation.
21 – Meditation and vibrational sound, the multidimensional sounds of nature.
22 – Visualized healing.
23 – Practicing continuum affirmations.
24 – Accessing and tuning into vibrational sounds.
25 – Reflections of the moment.
26 – Beyond the self.
27 – Who is the eternal I.
28 – Burning the past away.
29 – Accepting new manifestations.
30 – The Oneness of all in the

Interconnectedness.
31 –Meditation of kindness and lovingness.
32 –Our spinning core energy chakras.
33 –Your true nature revealed.
P 192-208 Chapter Four Accessing The Light Body, The MUNAY-KI Nine Rites Of Initiation.
P 209-214 Other books by LoveLifeLee.
P 215-225 Index Page, Legal Disclaimer, Two Poems, Chakra & Breathe image, back cover title.

Legal Disclaimer – If you have read any of my other twenty four books, you will know I have a wealth of knowledge, with an array of subjects, but my passion has been to pass ancient knowledge & widom about our Eternal Light Bodies by accessing the Schematic Blueprint within our DNA, to open are Human Angelic Light Body. So I have wrriten books that have discussed the functions of the mind and body, & Chemical reactions & Toxins in the body, and about

Psychoactive plants on the mind and body from my own lived experiences and from my knowledge of my Shamanic Practice of the Munay-Ki Nine Rites of initiation. Since a young age I have had the gift of intelligence with a rapid critical thinking mind, and able to critical research in depth, I have no medical qualifications, but from my books you can see I have studied in depth hundreds of thousands of subjects, I hope this knowledge is useful and helps anyone suffering from the indoctrination of the ideology and philosophy and Programming, from Mindset, or anyone who is in conflict with the dark shade of their Ego, or anyone interested in the Eight Principles of Geomancy, of Life or anyone looking to evolve into their Eternal Human Light Body, Namaste.

Blessings to the Oneness & all Sentient Beings Inside & Outside the Manifested Physical Realms, I Wish You Consciousness from my Heart Space, I Wish You Inner Peace to Project Outer Peace to bring Balance in the Cosmic Creation, the Brahman, the Whole.

I Wish you Enlightenment, I Wish you to step from Mortality to Immortality, I Wish You to Ascend to be fully Embodied but Travelling the Stars in the Hyper-Dimensional Matrix Energy Field., Transcending Time & Space, to be Teleporting, Quantum Leaping, Shapeshifting, Metamorphosising in Your True Nature of an Eternal Inter-Dimensional Divine Light being of Ultra Violet Cosmic Spirit Gravity Consciousness, for You are an Angel of Light, You are Goddesses & Gods of the Immortal Realm Outside Time & Space from the Source Eternal Kingdom of Light.

Blessings may Your Third Eye & Heart Space be Illuminated in the Divine Cosmic Energy of the Oneness, & Rise You Shall in Consciousness, Good Luck on Your Life Journey, & on Your Cosmic Journey Home to the Kingdom of Light. Love to You All, Namaste LoveLifeLee.

THE KEY TO BE FREE

Meditation is the key, meditation is the key the key to see all that be to access the eye of the mind, divine to perceive all that be, inter-dimensional meditation is the key, deeper and deeper I go silent I be, silence I be.

Then bang I'm free, light pours from the eye of the mind, bright it be wow that's me free to fly and soar I've opened a new door, a door to ascend to realms above and beyond to be free, to learn and grow multidimensionally, multidimensional I be, soaring to and fro to and fro I go.

Connected I be, to all I see infinitely floating in dimensions of light, lights so bright, radiating all colours that be down worm hole spirals, all my desires out the other side, floating in star systems I be infinitely, of new stars I see.

Floating in pink gases I be, through another porthole I go, at speeds of thought I see, then I arrived in the new cluster of stars as far as I can see, milky ways of the divine sublime it be, wow now I see, now I see I'm truly free.

THE HYPER DIMENSIONAL MATRIX

As we connect to the hyper-dimensional matrix, of energetic light, able to travel and transverse our way through wormholes creating torus fields to move through the vibrating waves of energy, dancing in light, photons, particles of light vibrating, in frequency in patterns creating forms and densities, we be our selfs, Conscious creating all that be, in forms and densities.

Travelling the web of life, we all be, only to realise the Oneness that we all be, one photon one particle of light, one Consciousness, one being, one Spirit intertwined divine illuminated, but expressing individually, some times the divine experience will be to learn and grow and create a beautiful manifestation, to manifest a Creation into being from love and light to shine bright in the Brahman, the Creation, the Whole.

This is the story for every Individual and United Soul, the multidimensional story of life, singing its song into being, scales high and low, vibrating high and low, slow and fast, loud and low, in all colours of the rainbow, the spectrum of all beauty, created by you and me beings of light, beautiful and bright, in the Oneness so bright, the Photon of light.

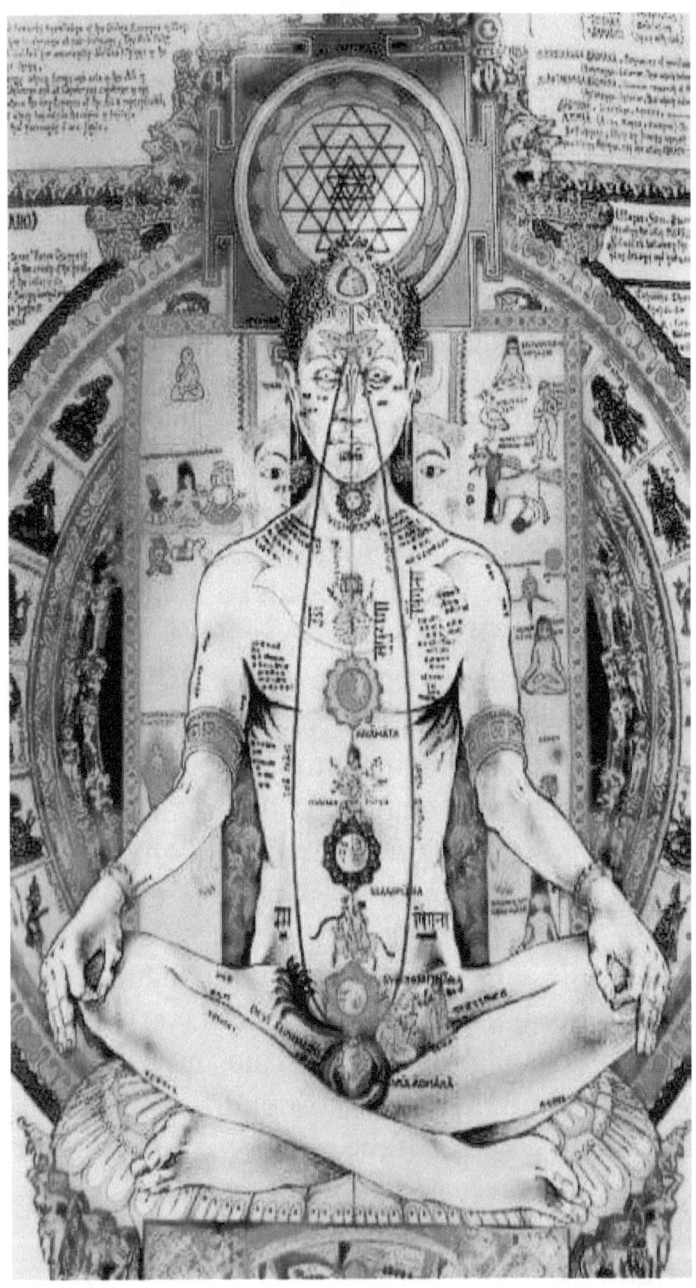

MEDITATION

IS THE KEY TO

YOUR WELL BEING

AND TO YOUR

MANIFESTED REALITY

THAT ENVOLOPES

SURROUNDS YOU

YOUR ENVIROMENT

This book discusses the Hidden Knowledge of Manifesting a New Mindset With the Eight Fundamental Principles of Geomancy, of the Creation, of Life, that come from Cosmic Universal Natural Law. Also discussed is the Great Work, the Introduction to the Angelic Human Eternal Light Body, that is accessed via higher states of Consciousness & by accessing your Schematic Blueprint within your DNA. There are many types of Meditation Practices in this book, of Ancient Wisdom & Knowledge from Worldwide Cultures, & gained in my own Meditation Practices, & from my Shamanic Ceremonies, & via Plant Medicines like Ayahuasca. There is focus on attention of the Unconscious Mind & Conscious Mind & their relationship, a concentration on Breath Work, & accessing your Light Body via your DNA Blueprint the Schematics to your Eternal Rainbow Light Body, accessed via Meditation, Breath, Diet, and your Consciousness.
Allowing you to access & travel in the Cosmos, in the Creation, in the Whole HyperDimensional Templar Light Time Matrix. Because we are Eternal Interdimensional Divine Light beings of Ultra Violet energetic Source Consciousness, we are the Christos Collective Cosmic Guardian's of the Creation.

www.ingramcontent.com/pod-product-compliance
Lightning Source LLC
Chambersburg PA
CBHW022059160426
43198CB00008B/280